barbecue

barbecue

delicious recipes for outdoor cooking

Louise Pickford photography by Ian Wallace

RYLAND
PETERS
& SMALL
LONDON NEW YORK

First published in Great Britain in 2003 as
Barbecue
This paperback edition first published in 2006
by Ryland Peters & Small
20–21 Jockey's Fields
London WC1R 4BW
www.rylandpeters.com

10 9 8 7 6 5 4 3 2

Printed in China

ISBN-10: 1 84597 082 9
ISBN-13: 978 1 84597 082 6

A CIP record for this book is available
from the British Library.

Senior Designers Steve Painter, Louise Leffler
Commissioning Editor Elsa Petersen-Schepelern
Editor Katherine Steer
Production Tamsin Curwood
Art Director Gabriella Le Grazie
Publishing Director Alison Starling

Food and Props Stylist Louise Pickford
Indexer Hilary Bird

Acknowledgements

Beautiful props were provided by The Baytree,
Woollahra, NSW; Bison Homewares,
Queanbeyan, ACT (www.bisonhome.com);
Camargue, Mosman, NSW; Tolle N Crowe,
Northbridge, NSW; Design Mode International,
Mona Vale, NSW; Village Living, Avalon NSW.
Above all, a big thank you to Weber Australia
for their help in supplying their huge range of
barbecues and equipment for the recipe
development and photography.
www.weberbbq.com.au

Notes

All spoon measurements are level unless
otherwise specified.

Uncooked or partly cooked eggs should not be
served to the very old or frail, the very young or
to pregnant women.

To sterilize preserving jars or bottles, wash the
jars in hot, soapy water and rinse in boiling
water. Put into a large saucepan and pour over
enough water to cover. With the lid on, bring the
water to the boil and continue boiling for
15 minutes. Turn off the heat, then leave the jars
in the hot water until just before they are to be
filled. Invert the jars onto clean kitchen paper to
dry. Sterilize the lids for 5 minutes by boiling.
Jars should be filled and sealed while still hot.

contents

barbecue ...

Today we associate barbecuing – or grilling as the Americans also call it – with being outdoors, and therefore countries with warmer climates tend to be better equipped for this type of cooking. Now I am based in Australia, it has become very attractive indeed. The result is this book – a celebration of outdoor cooking on the barbecue and I hope that by reading it and using the recipes, you will soon share my passion and enthusiasm for this age-old method of cooking.

The word 'barbecue' is derived from the Spanish word *barbacoa* and has several meanings: one is to cook over dry heat, such as coals; another is the equipment on which this is done; and a third is the meal itself – sometimes something as grand as a party. It seems to have originated in the Caribbean and Florida, then migrated across America's Deep South where barbecuing became a way of life. Barbecues as social gatherings can be traced back to when plantation owners held massive barbecues for friends, families and indeed their slaves.

Most of us are never going to barbecue on that scale, so the recipes in this book have been designed accordingly. I have included several recipes for which you will need a barbecue with a lid, such as a Weber, so the method is a little like using a conventional oven. If you don't have one like this, I apologize, but you will find that the majority of recipes here can be cooked in the normal way on either a gas or charcoal grill.

Which is best – charcoal or gas? Having tested these recipes using both types, I can offer an opinion. For flavour I would choose a charcoal barbecue, but for convenience the gas version wins hands down, especially if you are cooking for two. Imagine heating the coals for up to 40 minutes, then searing a tuna steak for one minute on each side. Of course, I realize you can buy small charcoal barbecues where you need only heat up a few coals, but turning a dial and pressing the ignite button on a gas barbecue for almost instant heat is far more efficient and appealing. The same argument might apply to electric barbecues, but I really think cooking on one of these is a bit like cooking on a regular stove. For a barbecue, we need fire!

I think that today, for many of us, barbecuing has become one of our preferred methods of cooking, as well as a very enjoyable way of entertaining. It is a great way to cook, not only for the flavour of the food, but because it's done outdoors and, more often than not, involves a small gathering of friends and family where everyone can chip in, have fun and eat great dishes.

Oh yes, in case I forget, I hear that, as tradition would have it, we girls can sit back and chill while the men get busy with the cookin'.

barbecue practicalities

Which barbecue?

There are three main categories of barbecue to choose from: charcoal/wood, gas or electric.

Charcoal barbecues, designed to burn both coals and wood, are messy to use, take a long time to prepare and need constant attention, but the food has that distinctive smoky caramelized flavour we love so much. The exterior of the food is sticky and char-grilled while the interior remains moist and succulent.

Gas, on the other hand, can be lit in seconds and the temperature set with the twist of a dial. It is easy to clean with no hot coals to worry about at the end. Most gas barbecues have a flat plate as well as a regular grill so you can cook every cut of meat or type of fish with ease, and if you're cooking for just one or two people, they can save you time and money. The end result will taste good but may not have that char-grilled flavour of charcoal or wood.

Food cooked on an electric barbecue will also lack that special smoky taste, but this style of barbecue does have the advantage of being usable where one with an open flame would not be suitable – in high-rise buildings, for example, or on days of total fire ban.

Weighing up the choices, it seems that the ideal solution is to have several kinds on hand (you don't need to spend a great deal to get a good-quality gas or charcoal barbecue). This is for two reasons; first, if you are cooking for just one or two people, gas is probably a more sensible option – or, if I'm cooking for a larger crowd, I prefer to cook over coals when it's worth the extra effort.

Choosing a charcoal barbecue

The **disposable barbecue** sets available from many supermarkets or hardware stores are ideal for the 'once-in-a-while' barbecue.

The highly **portable barbecues**, such as the cast-iron Hibachi from Japan (available worldwide), are small and relatively inexpensive. They are usually vented to help to increase or decrease the heat or have a rung system above the coals so the grill rack can be low or high as necessary.

The **table barbecue** is really a box on legs. The box, called a grate, takes the coals, with the grill rack for cooking set above that. Again the rack can be raised higher or lower as necessary. This type of barbecue is commonplace in some countries and is mostly used for direct grilling. Some are available with lids. Make sure the legs are sturdy before buying this type of barbecue.

Kettle barbecues, such as Weber, are very versatile, great for both direct and indirect grilling (page 11).

The kettle-shaped drum protects the fire from wind or rain and the dome-shaped lid transforms it into an oven. The vent system on a kettle barbecue also makes it easier to control the temperature – wide-open vents create a hotter fire, while closed vents will extinguish it.

Choosing a gas barbecue

Available in all shapes, sizes and prices – just decide how often you will use it, how many people you will cook for, and exactly what you want your barbecue to do.

The cheapest is the **simple gas barbecue**, again shaped like a table with gas burners rather than charcoal. It usually has both a flat plate and a grill section and is best suited to direct grilling because it has no lid.

Middle-range gas barbecues will have a lid and often have side attachments, including shelves.

The **gas barbecue on wheels** has a dome-shaped lid and may include side attachments such as shelves for stacking plates, or an extra round burner designed to hold a wok. It may have a thermometer device and a rotisserie attachment. It can be used for direct and indirect grilling, smoking and rotisserie cooking.

Top-end super-barbecues include 'everything but the kitchen sink' for the true barbecue enthusiast. Often made in stainless steel, they are quite magnificent and will include all the mod cons mentioned earlier, plus a separate smoker box.

Choosing an electric barbecue

There are several electric barbecues on the market and although they don't give the flame-grilled flavour produced by gas, charcoal or wood, they still have appeal. When buying an electric barbecue always check that the legs are sturdy and that it has a thermostat. The special advantages are:
• Ideal for a deck area where sparks could be dangerous and particularly suited to high-rise living.
• Easily regulated with a thermostat for accurate and instant temperature control.
• Great for impromptu cooking.
• Some can be used for smoking.

Building your own barbecue

A homemade barbecue can be a DIY construction of bricks, a store-bought grill top and some charcoal – or it could be a virtual outdoor kitchen.

Before you start, decide what type of barbecue you need, the size you want and the location. If you want a more sophisticated affair, consult the professionals.

Fuels

Charcoal
There are two main types of charcoal to choose from.
• **Charcoal briquettes** are the most common, and available from supermarkets and hardware stores. However, check with your local specialty barbecue supplier, because some briquettes can contain added chemicals.

• **Hardwood lump** charcoal is not so widely available, but try larger suppliers or specialists (see Websites, page 142). Made from whole logs burned in a kiln before being broken into chunks, it contains no additives, burns easily, heats quickly and lasts well.

Gas
Gas bottles are transportable, but if you are always going to barbecue at home in the same spot, then it may be worth having your barbecue adapted so it can be connected straight into the gas supply (some barbecues are supplied with an adaptor). Check with your local gas supplier and a qualified plumber.
• Gas bottles in different sizes are widely available from petrol stations, hardware stores and barbecue suppliers. You pay a deposit on the bottle, which can be exchanged for a full one whenever necessary.

charcoal briquettes

lumpwood charcoal

wood chunks

wood chips

Wood

Wood is the original fuel used to create fire and is the preferred option for many as it adds a more intense flavour to foods. It can be harder to find than charcoal and is often a more expensive choice.

• Wood chunks are better, and they are available from larger barbecue suppliers.
• Wood chips are smaller pieces of the same wood, but these are used to create extra smoke for flavour.
• Use only hardwoods such as hickory, oak, apple and olive wood. Mesquite, if available, is excellent.
• Never use softwoods, because they can produce excess soot and too much smoke.

A chimney starter is an easy and efficient way to light the coals for the barbecue

Use a taper or long match to light the firelighters, which will light the charcoal

getting started

Lighting charcoal by hand

• Arrange the charcoal 10 cm deep in the middle of the grate, and put a few firelighters between the coals. Light the firelighters and leave the coals for 40–45 minutes until they are glowing red and covered in a light grey ash. You can also use a chimney starter (right).
• Rake the coals over the surface of the grate leaving a small area uncovered so there is a cool spot you can move the cooked meat to. If more than one temperature is needed, rake some coals on top of each other so there is a double layer. This will be the hottest region, while the single layer of coals will have a medium heat.
• The coals should now stay hot for up to one hour, cooling gradually.

Lighting charcoal with a chimney starter

A chimney starter is a metal cylinder with a handle and a wire partition inside to hold the charcoal. It is used to heat the charcoal before it is tipped out onto the grate. Available from larger suppliers.
• Wad some newspaper and put it in the base of the chimney. Fill the chimney with charcoal. Light the newspaper and leave for 20 minutes until the charcoal is glowing orange.
• Use an oven mitt to lift the chimney and release the charcoal onto the grate. Leave for 10 minutes until the coals are covered in a light ash. They are now ready.
• If you are planning to cook a large amount of food, or or will be cooking for longer than one hour, prepare additional charcoal in the same way.

Lighting wood

• To light wood without a chimney starter, put a few small dry twigs on the grate with a few firelighters. Add a good heap of wood chunks, light the firelighters, and leave the wood to burn until it is glowing and ashen and no flames remain.
• Alternatively pile wood chunks into a chimney starter and follow the method for lighting coals (above).

Temperature guide

• To test the heat, hold your hand 12 cm above the fire and count how long you can comfortably keep it there. For a hot fire, it will be about 2 seconds, a medium-hot fire 3–4 seconds, and a cool fire 5–6 seconds.
• Some barbecues have adjustable racks to adjust the height of the grill rack to achieve the correct temperature.

Cooking methods on a charcoal or wood barbecue

Direct grilling
This is the most common cooking method where the food is cooked directly over a high heat (between 200–250°C) to give it that wonderful char-grilled flavour.
• When the coals are hot and have been raked to their required position, use oil to spray the grill rack away from the heat, then replace the grill rack over the coals.
• Leave for 5 minutes while the grill rack heats up – the food will be less likely to stick.
• Put the food onto the grill rack and cook on both sides until ready – the time will vary from recipe to recipe.

Indirect grilling
This method is for cooking food over a lower heat for a longer period and is ideal for larger pieces of meat or fatty cuts of meat, such as ribs or duck breast. It is only used if you have a grill with a lid. The coals or wood are separated leaving a cooler spot in the middle with a drip tray underneath.
• When the coals are ready, rake them into two piles at either side of the grill and put a drip tray in the middle.
• Remove the grill rack and use oil to spray or brush it, making sure to point it away from the heat before returning it over the coals.
• Put the food into the middle of the grill rack directly over the drip tray. Cover with a lid and cook as required.

Cooking methods on a gas barbecue

Direct grilling
• About 20 minutes before you start to cook, fire up the barbecue according to the manufacturer's instructions. Let it heat up, then turn the dial to the heat you require.
• Carefully spray or brush the grill rack or flat plate with oil.
• It is now ready for cooking.

Indirect grilling
You can grill indirectly just as easily with gas, providing it has at least 2 burners. Gas barbecues come with a drip tray already in place in the middle of the grill but below the burners.
• Fire up the barbecue and, if you have two burners, leave only one of them lit. If you have a three-burner barbecue, light the two outer burners, and if you have a four-burner barbecue, again light the outer two and leave the central burners unlit.
• Carefully spray or brush the middle of the grill rack with oil (take care – there may be flare-ups) and put the food above the unlit burner.

Smoking and smokers

Smoking is done using the indirect grilling method so the food cooks more slowly and the flavour of the smoke can penetrate. For smoking you will need a barbecue with a lid. If you have either a home smoker or a barbecue with a smoker attachment, follow the manufacturer's instructions.

Smoking over coals
• Arrange the coals in the grate as for indirect grilling (see above).
• Soak about 125 g of wood chips in cold water for at least 1 hour.
• When the coals are ready to use, drain the wood chips and shake off any excess water. Put half the chips onto each pile of coals and wait until they start to smoke.
• Working away from the heat, spray or brush the rack with oil before returning it to the barbecue.
• As soon as the chips start to smoke, put the food directly over the drip tray in the middle of the grill rack and top with the lid.

Smoking over gas
Although the results with gas are not as good as with charcoal, you can still smoke on a gas barbecue, providing it has a lid.
• Set up the barbecue for indirect grilling (above).

• Soak about 125 g of wood chips in cold water for at least 1 hour.
• Preheat the barbecue for about 20 minutes and then reduce the heat to medium.
• When the coals are ready to use, drain the wood chips and shake off any excess water.
• Put the chips on a piece of foil, fold the foil over, and turn the edges under to seal the package. Pierce about 10 holes in the top.
• Put the foil package directly on one of the burners underneath the grill rack.
• As soon as smoke appears, put the food in the centre of the oiled rack, cover with the lid and cook for the specified time.

Smoking over wood

Using wood will naturally give the food more flavour, but you can increase this by adding soaked wood chips just before cooking. Follow the instructions for indirect grilling and smoking over coals, above.

Equipment

The following items are recommended for safe and successful grilling.
• A **chimney starter** (page 10) is a metal cylinder used to light the charcoal before putting on the barbecue.
• I find that a **small garden hoe** with a handle about 1 metre long is the ideal tool for raking hot coals safely across the barbecue. You need something with a long handle, to keep your hands away from the heat.

• An **oil spray** is ideal for spraying both the grill rack and flat plate, as well as for spraying food items before barbecuing.
• A **basting brush** is used for basting the food as it cooks. This can be a simple pastry brush.
• A good-quality **wire brush** for cleaning the grill rack.
• **Aluminium foil** trays available from supermarkets and hardware stores make ideal drip trays for charcoal barbecues.
• Wooden handled **tongs** for turning the meat. If your tongs have a metal handle, then always use a thick oven mitt to hold them.
• A good-quality thick **oven mitt** – handling hot utensils with damp cloths is a sure way to scald yourself.
• **Metal skewers** for kebabs, but remember to use an oven mitt when handling hot metal.
• **Wooden or bamboo skewers** are great for kebabs but must always be pre-soaked in cold water to prevent them from burning.
• If you plan to cook larger pieces of meat, buy an **instant-read meat thermometer** so you can test the internal temperature.
• A **stove-top grill pan** is useful as an alternative to a flat plate if you have a charcoal barbecue.
• A **grill basket** will be useful if you are are going to cook whole fish or fish fillets, as these can sometimes stick, even if the grill is well oiled. The fish are contained within the basket which is turned half-way through cooking.

• A **portable light** which can be hung up outside over the cooking area is very useful.
• **Insect repellent** is very useful, and it is also a good idea to burn citronella candles or mosquito coils.
• **Night lights** and other outdoor candles will add both light and ambience to an evening barbecue.

Cleaning

Cleaning methods for charcoal and gas barbecues are the same.
• Use a wire brush to rub off any cooked-on debris from the grill rack.
• The best time to clean the grill rack is directly after cooking while it is still hot. Use a wire brush to rub off as much debris as possible.
• Brush or spray the grill rack with oil before cooking to prevent sticking.
• Let the grill rack heat well before adding the food. This will help to prevent the food from sticking.
• Brush or spray the grill rack with oil after cleaning to help to stop rust.
• Always cover the barbecue with a lid or a waterproof sheet when it is not being used.

little dishes for the grill

Firing up the grill is always exciting, because we know it will produce delicious foods with that lovely smoky, char-grilled flavour. We usually grill for a group of people rather than just one or two, so I thought it would be a good idea to put together a selection of small dishes you can prepare in advance, so you can spread them out on a large table for everyone to share.

Most of these little dishes will also work well as starters to whet the appetite while the main course marinates for a few minutes longer. Alternatively, if you increase the quantities, some of the recipes could also be served as a main course, such as the Pepper 'n' Spice Chicken (page 19). Simply double the quantities as required.

If you would rather serve starters that need little or no cooking on the grill, all the recipes can be easily cooked in the kitchen on a stove-top grill pan or under the grill.

This dish is similar to the famous Peking duck, but minus the time it takes to prepare it. Cooking duck on the barbecue is best done by the indirect grilling method (page 11) where the coals are pushed to the sides and a drip tray placed underneath to catch the fat.

barbecue duck ricepaper rolls

2 duck breast fillets, about 200 g each

1 tablespoon salt

2 tablespoons honey

2 tablespoons dark soy sauce

½ teaspoon ground star anise

12 package Vietnamese ricepaper wrappers (*bahn trang*)*

½ cucumber, cut into strips

a few fresh herb leaves, such as coriander, mint and Thai basil

Asian Barbecue Sauce, to serve (page 116)

serves 4

Ricepaper wrappers are sold in packets of 50 or 100. Seal leftovers in the same packet, put in a plastic bag and seal well.

Using a sharp knife, cut several slashes into the duck skin. Rub the skin with the salt and put in a shallow dish. Put the honey, soy sauce and ground star anise into a bowl and mix well. Pour over the duck. Let marinate in a cool place for at least 1 hour.

Set up the barbecue for indirect grilling (page 11) and put a drip tray in the middle. Cook the duck breast for 15 minutes or until well browned and firm to the touch, let rest for 5 minutes, then cut into thin strips and set aside until required.

Put the ricepaper wrappers into a large bowl of cold water, let soak until softened, then pat dry and spread flat on the work surface. Put a few slices of duck, some strips of cucumber and herbs into the middle of each wrapper and add a little of the barbecue sauce.

Fold the ends of the wrapper over the duck and roll up the sides to enclose the filling. Transfer to a large platter and serve with the barbecue sauce.

pepper 'n' spice chicken

Based on the classic Asian salt 'n' pepper squid, this delicious dish came about one day when I was playing around with a few spices and some chicken I had left over. It's now a family favourite. Serve with a squeeze of lime and chilli sauce.

1 small chicken

1 recipe Fragrant Asian Rub (page 121)

2 tablespoons toasted sesame oil

1–2 limes, cut into wedges

Sweet Chilli Sauce (page 116), to serve

serves 4

Cut the chicken into 12 portions and put into a dish. Add the rub and sesame oil and work well into the chicken pieces. Let marinate in the refrigerator for 2 hours, but return to room temperature for 1 hour before cooking.

Preheat the barbecue, then cook the chicken over medium hot coals for 15–20 minutes, turning after 10 minutes, until the chicken is cooked through and the juices run clear when the thickest part of the meat is pierced with a skewer. Squeeze with lime juice, let cool slightly and serve with the Sweet Chilli Sauce.

Gooey, caramelized garlic spread over lightly char-grilled toast is the perfect starter to amuse your guests while you cook the main course. It tastes absolutely amazing!

bruschetta with caramelized garlic

1 whole head of garlic

a sprig of fresh thyme

1 tablespoon extra virgin olive oil, plus extra to sprinkle

4 slices sourdough or ciabatta bread

sea salt and freshly ground black pepper

serves 4

Cut the top off the garlic head to reveal the cloves. Put the head onto a piece of foil, add the thyme sprig and season with salt and pepper. Sprinkle with the olive oil, then fold over the foil, sealing the edges to form a parcel.

Preheat the barbecue, then cook over hot coals for about 20 minutes or until the garlic is softened.

Put the bread slices on the grill rack and toast for a few minutes on each side. Squeeze the cooked garlic out of the cloves and spread onto the toasted bread. Sprinkle with a little more olive oil, season with salt and pepper and serve while still warm.

Variation

Try topping the garlic with slices of Camembert cheese and sprinkle with extra virgin olive oil.

Panini, which is Italian for toasted sandwiches can be prepared ahead of time, then cooked just before you want to serve them. The combination of char-grilled peppers, tender chicken and a delicious rocket aïoli is definitely hard to beat.

chicken panini
with roasted pepper and rocket aïoli

2 red peppers, left whole

4 small focaccia or Turkish rolls, halved

2 large, cooked chicken breasts, shredded

a small handful of baby spinach

rocket aïoli

1 egg yolk

1 teaspoon white wine vinegar

a bunch of rocket, about 50 g, coarsely chopped

1 garlic clove, crushed

150 ml olive oil

sea salt and freshly ground black pepper

serves 4

Preheat the barbecue, then cook the peppers over hot coals or grill for about 20 minutes until charred all over. Put into a plastic bag and let cool. Peel off the skin and discard the seeds, then cut the flesh into strips.

To make the aïoli, put the egg yolk, vinegar and a little salt and pepper into a food processor and blend briefly until frothy. Add the rocket and garlic and pulse for 30 seconds. With the machine still running, gradually pour in the olive oil until the sauce is thickened and speckled with vivid green. Taste and adjust the seasoning.

Spread a little of the rocket aïoli onto the cut sides of each roll and fill the rolls with the chicken, pepper strips and spinach leaves. Press the halves together.

Preheat the flat plate on the barbecue and cook the panini over low heat for 4–5 minutes, then, using tongs, flip over and cook the other side for a further 5 minutes until toasted. If you don't have a flat plate, cook on a stove-top grill pan, either on the barbecue, or on the stove. Serve hot.

This combination may sound slightly unusual, but it is in fact totally delicious. Fresh oysters, a nibble of the hot sausages and a sip of chilled white wine is a taste sensation – try it, you'll be amazed.

oysters with spicy chorizo

2 spicy chorizo sausages

20 freshly shucked oysters

dry white wine, to serve

shallot vinegar

3 tablespoons red wine vinegar

2 tablespoons finely chopped shallot

1 tablespoon snipped fresh chives

sea salt and freshly ground black pepper

cocktail sticks

a large platter filled with a layer of ice cubes

serves 4

To make the shallot vinegar, put the ingredients into a bowl and mix well. Pour into a small dish and set aside until required.

Preheat the barbecue, then cook the sausages over hot coals for 8–10 minutes or until cooked through. Cut the sausages into bite-sized pieces and spike them onto cocktail sticks. Arrange in the centre of a large serving platter filled with ice. Put the oysters into their half-shells and arrange on the ice. Serve with the shallot vinegar.

Serving a large platter of grilled vegetables provides a lovely start to any barbecue – just choose a combination of your favourites. A delicious way to serve them is on a bed of Grilled Polenta.

vegetable antipasto

2 red peppers

4 baby fennel bulbs

1 large aubergine

2 large courgettes

1 red onion

1 recipe Herb, Lemon and Garlic Marinade (page 118)

a few fresh herb leaves, such as basil, dill, fennel, mint and parsley

extra virgin olive oil, to taste

lemon juice, to taste

sea salt and freshly ground black pepper

bread or Grilled Polenta (page 104), to serve

serves 4

Cut the peppers into quarters and remove and discard the seeds. Trim the fennel, reserving the fronds, and cut the bulbs into 5 mm slices. Cut the aubergine into thick slices and cut in half again. Cut the courgettes into thick slices diagonally and cut the onion into wedges.

Put all the vegetables into a large bowl, add the marinade and toss gently until evenly coated. Let marinate in a cool place for at least 1 hour.

Preheat the barbecue, then cook the vegetables on the grill rack until they are all tender and lightly charred. Let cool, then peel the peppers.

Arrange the vegetables on a large platter, sprinkle with the herbs, reserved fennel fronds, olive oil and lemon juice, then season lightly with salt and pepper.

Serve at room temperature with crusty bread or grilled polenta triangles.

Satays are found all over South-east Asia. They are very easy to make and taste simply wonderful.

prawn and beef satays

20 uncooked prawns

250 g fillet steak

dipping sauces, to serve

prawn marinade

1 teaspoon coriander seeds

½ teaspoon cumin seeds

1 garlic clove, crushed

1 teaspoon grated fresh ginger

2 kaffir lime leaves, shredded

1 teaspoon ground turmeric

1 tablespoon light soy sauce

4 tablespoons coconut milk

½ teaspoon salt

beef marinade

1 garlic clove, crushed

2 stalks of lemongrass, trimmed and finely chopped

1 tablespoon grated fresh ginger

4 coriander roots, finely chopped

1 red chilli, finely chopped

grated zest and juice of 1 lime

1 tablespoon Thai fish sauce

1 tablespoon dark soy sauce

1½ tablespoons sugar

1 tablespoon sesame oil

freshly ground black pepper

40 wooden skewers soaked in cold water for 30 minutes

serves 4

Shell and devein the prawns, wash them under cold running water and pat dry with kitchen paper. Put them into a shallow dish.

To make the prawn marinade, put the coriander and cumin seeds into a dry frying pan and toast over medium heat until golden and aromatic. Remove, let cool slightly, then transfer to a spice grinder (or clean coffee grinder). Add the garlic, ginger and lime leaves and grind to a coarse paste. Alternatively, use a mortar and pestle.

Transfer to a bowl, add the turmeric, soy sauce, coconut milk and salt and mix well. Pour over the prawns and let marinate in the refrigerator for 1 hour.

To make the beef satays, cut the fillet steak across the grain into thin strips. Mix all the beef marinade ingredients in a shallow dish, add the beef strips and let marinate for about 1 hour.

Preheat the barbecue. To assemble the beef satays, thread the beef strips onto the skewers, zig-zagging back and forth as you go. To assemble the prawn satays, thread the prawns lengthways onto the skewers.

Cook both kinds of satays over hot coals for 2 minutes each side, brushing the beef marinade over the beef satays half-way through. Serve hot with your choice of dipping sauces.

Ripe figs filled with goats' cheese, then wrapped in prosciutto make a great first course. Prepare the salad in advance, but add the dressing at the last minute, otherwise it may become soggy.

fig, goats' cheese and prosciutto skewers with radicchio salad

8 large ripe figs

80 g goats' cheese

8 slices prosciutto

radicchio salad

1 head of radicchio, trimmed

a handful of walnut pieces, pan-toasted

4 tablespoons walnut oil

2 tablespoon extra virgin olive oil

1 tablespoon vincotto or Reduced Balsamic Vinegar*

sea salt and freshly ground black pepper

4 wooden skewers soaked in cold water for 30 minutes

serves 4

Using a sharp knife, cut each fig lengthways into quarters without cutting all the way through. Cut the cheese into 8 equal pieces, put into the middle of each fig and close the figs. Wrap each fig with a slice of the ham and thread carefully onto the soaked wooden skewers.

Preheat the barbecue, then cook the skewers over medium hot coals for 4–5 minutes, turning half-way through until the ham is charred and the figs are sizzling.

To make the salad, tear the radicchio leaves into pieces and put into a bowl with the walnuts. Put the remaining ingredients into a separate bowl and whisk well. Pour the dressing over the leaves and toss until coated. Serve with the skewers.

*Note To reduce balsamic vinegar, put 300 ml into a saucepan and boil gently until reduced by about two-thirds and has reached the consistency of thick syrup. Let cool, then store in a clean jar or bottle.

salads and vegetables

Salads are always a welcome addition to a barbecue. They add a lovely freshness to the meal as well as colour and texture. Although all the salad recipes in this book require grilling for some part of the dish, you can always use your stove-top grill pan or kitchen grill beforehand if you prefer.

Vegetables are perfect for cooking on the grill because they need little preparation. You can use a simple marinade or just brush with seasoned oil – in a few moments they will be transformed into some of the most deliciously sweet morsels you can imagine.

I can't think of any vegetable that is unsuited to grilling and I have from time to time cooked everything from the humble potato (great cooked in the embers of the fire, page 37) to artichokes, asparagus and even broccoli. A selection of vegetables makes a colourful centrepiece to any table and they can be served as either an accompaniment to a meat or fish dish or as a starter.

This satisfying summer salad with a delicious hint of fresh mint makes a superb accompaniment to barbecued meat or fish.

courgette, feta and mint salad

1 tablespoon sesame seeds

6 large courgettes

3 tablespoons extra virgin olive oil

150 g feta cheese, crumbled

a handful of fresh mint leaves

dressing

4 tablespoons extra virgin olive oil

1 tablespoon lemon juice

1 small garlic clove, crushed

sea salt and freshly ground black pepper

serves 4

Put the sesame seeds into a dry frying pan and toast over medium heat until golden and aromatic. Remove from the heat, let cool and set aside until required.

Preheat the barbecue. Cut the courgettes diagonally into thick slices, toss with the olive oil and season with salt and pepper. Cook over hot coals for 2–3 minutes on each side until charred and tender. Remove and let cool.

Put all the dressing ingredients into a screw-top jar and shake well. Add salt and pepper to taste.

Put the courgettes, feta and mint into a large bowl, add the dressing and toss well until evenly coated. Sprinkle with the sesame seeds and serve at once.

When I was a child we would bury foil-wrapped potatoes in the embers of the bonfire on Guy Fawkes Night and by the time the fireworks were over, our jacket potatoes were cooked to perfection – a crispy skin with soft, fluffy insides.

ember-roasted potatoes

4 medium roasting potatoes, such as King Edward or Desirée

butter

sea salt and freshly ground black pepper

serves 4

Wrap the potatoes individually in a double layer of foil and, as soon as the coals are glowing red, put the potatoes on top. Rake the charcoal up and around them, but without covering them. Let cook for about 25 minutes, then using tongs, turn the potatoes over carefully and cook for a further 25–30 minutes until cooked through.

Remove from the heat and carefully remove the foil, then cut the potatoes in half. Serve, topped with a spoonful of butter, salt and pepper.

Variation

To cook sweet potatoes, follow the same method but cook for about 20 minutes on each side.

½ red onion, sliced

6 sweet red peppers

500 g asparagus spears, trimmed

extra virgin olive oil, for brushing

250 g mangetout

75 g mixed salad leaves

a handful of fresh parsley and dill leaves

50 g hazelnuts, toasted and coarsely chopped

hazelnut oil dressing

4 tablespoons hazelnut oil

2 tablespoons extra virgin olive oil

1 tablespoon sherry vinegar

1 teaspoon caster sugar

sea salt and freshly ground black pepper

serves 4–6

Vegetables taste wonderful when cooked on the barbecue – it brings out their natural sweetness. Look out for the long, thin red peppers (ramiro or romano) when available – they are particularly good grilled. This salad serves four as a main course or six as a starter.

salad of roasted peppers and asparagus

Put the sliced onion into a sieve, sprinkle with salt and let drain over a bowl for 30 minutes. Rinse under cold running water and pat dry with kitchen paper.

Preheat the barbecue, then cook the peppers over hot coals for 15 minutes, turning frequently until charred all over. Transfer to a plastic bag, seal and let soften until cool. Peel off the skin and discard the seeds, then cut the flesh into thick strips.

Brush the asparagus with olive oil and cook over hot coals for 3–4 minutes, turning frequently, until charred and tender.

Put the mangetout into a large saucepan of lightly salted boiling water and boil for 1–2 minutes. Drain and refresh under cold running water.

Put the onion, peppers, asparagus and mangetout into a large bowl and toss gently. Add the salad leaves, herbs and hazelnuts. Put the dressing ingredients into a bowl and whisk well, then pour over the salad and toss until coated. Serve.

To cook these delicious cakes you will need a barbecue with a flat plate. Alternatively, you can use a flat griddle or heavy-based frying pan preheated over the hot coals. Either way, they taste absolutely wonderful.

sweetcorn griddle cakes

400 g canned corn kernels, drained

65 g polenta

50 g plain flour

1 teaspoon baking powder

½ teaspoon bicarbonate of soda

½ teaspoon salt

150 ml buttermilk

1 tablespoon vegetable oil

½ large free range egg

olive oil, for spraying

to serve

smoked salmon

crème fraîche

salmon caviar

serves 4

Put half the corn into a food processor and process until fairly smooth. Add the polenta, flour, baking powder, bicarbonate of soda, salt, buttermilk, vegetable oil and egg and blend to form a thick batter. Transfer to a bowl and stir in the remaining corn.

Preheat the flat plate on your barbecue to low and spray with olive oil. Spoon on the batter to make 4 cakes, 10 cm diameter and cook for 2 minutes. Using a spatula, flip and cook for a further 30 seconds or until golden on both sides and firm to the touch. If you don't have a flat plate, use a heavy flat griddle or frying pan, either on the barbecue, or on the stove. Transfer to a plate and keep the corn cakes warm.

Repeat to make 8 cakes. Serve, topped with smoked salmon, crème fraîche and salmon caviar.

Fatoush is a bread salad made from grilled pita bread. It's often accompanied by haloumi, a firm cheese that can be char-grilled. Fresh mozzarella cheese can also be cooked on the grill. It picks up an appealing smokiness in the process.

250 g fresh mozzarella cheese, drained

1 large green pepper, deseeded and chopped

1 Lebanese (mini) cucumber, chopped

2 ripe tomatoes, chopped

1/2 red onion, finely chopped

2 pita breads

4 tablespoons extra virgin olive oil

freshly squeezed juice of 1/2 lemon

sea salt and freshly ground black pepper

olive salsa

75 g Kalamata olives, pitted and chopped

1 tablespoon chopped fresh parsley

1 small garlic clove, finely chopped

4 tablespoons extra virgin olive oil

1 tablespoon lemon juice

freshly cracked black pepper

serves 4

grilled pita salad
with olive salsa and mozzarella

Wrap the mozzarella in kitchen paper and squeeze to remove excess water. Unwrap and cut into thick slices. Brush the slices well with olive oil. Cook over the hot coals for 1 minute on each side until the cheese is charred with lines and beginning to soften. Alternatively, simply slice the cheese and use without grilling.

Put the green pepper, cucumber, tomatoes and onion into a bowl. Toast the pita breads over hot coals, cool slightly, then tear into bite-sized pieces. Add to the bowl, then pour over the olive oil and lemon juice. Season and stir well.

Put all the ingredients for the olive salsa into a bowl and stir well.

Spoon the salad onto small plates, top with a few slices of mozzarella and some olive salsa, then serve.

This is just one of those dishes I make over and over again, particularly in the summer when tomatoes are so good. For the best flavour, use vine-ripened tomatoes. If sourdough bread is unavailable, use ciabatta instead.

tomato and grilled bread salad

4 slices sourdough bread

2 garlic cloves, peeled but left whole

8 tablespoons extra virgin olive oil

650 g vine-ripened tomatoes, coarsely chopped

50 g pitted black olives

1 tablespoon aged balsamic vinegar

a handful of fresh basil, leaves torn

sea salt and freshly ground black pepper

serves 4–6

Preheat the barbecue, then grill the bread slices over hot coals for 1 minute on each side or until toasted and charred. Remove from the heat, rub all over with the garlic, then sprinkle with 2 tablespoons of the oil. Let cool, then cut into cubes.

Put the grilled bread into a large bowl and add the tomatoes and olives. Put the remaining olive oil and vinegar into a separate bowl and mix well, then pour over the salad. Season with salt and pepper and stir well.

Set aside to infuse for 30 minutes, then stir in the basil leaves and serve.

Orzo is a rice-shaped pasta, ideal for making into a salad because it retains its shape and texture really well after cooking.

orzo salad
with lemon and herb dressing

250 g cherry tomatoes, halved

6 tablespoons extra virgin olive oil

250 g orzo or other tiny soup pasta*

6 spring onions, finely chopped

4 tablespoons coarsely chopped mixed fresh herbs, such as basil, dill, mint and parsley

grated zest and juice of 2 unwaxed lemons

sea salt and freshly ground black pepper

4 wooden skewers, soaked in cold water for 30 minutes

serves 4

Preheat the barbecue or griller. Thread the tomatoes onto the soaked wooden skewers with all the cut halves facing the same way. Sprinkle with a little olive oil, season with salt and pepper and cook over hot coals or under the grill for 1–2 minutes on each side until lightly charred and softened. Remove from the heat and set aside.

Bring a large saucepan of lightly salted water to the boil. Add the orzo and cook for about 9 minutes or until *al dente*. Drain well and transfer to a large bowl.

Heat 2 tablespoons of the olive oil in a frying pan, add the onions, herbs and lemon zest and stir-fry for 30 seconds. Stir into the orzo, then add the tomatoes, lemon juice, remaining olive oil, salt and pepper. Toss well and let cool before using.

*Note Orzo is available from many large supermarkets and Italian delicatessens. If unavailable, use other pasta shapes instead.

grilled corn-on-the-cob

In this version of the famous recipe, corn-on-the-cob steams inside the husks first, then has a short blast over the hot coals to brown and flavour the kernels. Delicious served with plenty of crusty bread to mop up the juices.

4 corn cobs, unhusked

125 g butter

1 garlic clove, crushed

2 teaspoons chopped fresh thyme

grated zest of 1 unwaxed lemon

sea salt and freshly ground black pepper

crusty bread, to serve

serves 4

Carefully peel back the husks from the corn, but leave them attached at the stalk. Remove and discard the cornsilk. Fold the husks back in position and tie in place with string. Put the corn in a large bowl of cold water, let soak for 30 minutes, then drain and pat dry with kitchen paper.

Preheat the barbecue, then cook the corn over medium hot coals for 15 minutes, turning regularly until the outer husks are evenly charred. Remove from the heat, let cool slightly, then remove the husks. Return to the grill rack and cook for a further 8–10 minutes, turning frequently until the kernels are lightly charred.

Meanwhile, put the butter, garlic, thyme, lemon zest, salt and pepper into a small saucepan and heat gently until the butter has melted. Sprinkle the butter mixture over the cooked corn and serve with crusty bread.

For this dish, you need beetroot and baby onions of roughly the same size, so they will cook evenly on the barbecue. An excellent accompaniment to grilled meats or salads.

beetroot and baby onion brochettes

32 large fresh bay leaves

20 small beetroot

20 baby onions, unpeeled

3 tablespoons extra virgin olive oil

1 tablespoon balsamic vinegar

sea salt and freshly ground black pepper

8 metal skewers

serves 4

Put the bay leaves into a bowl, cover with cold water and let soak for 1 hour before cooking.

Cut the stalks off the beetroot and wash well under cold running water. Put the beetroot and baby onions into a large saucepan of lightly salted boiling water and blanch for 5 minutes. Drain and refresh under cold running water. Pat dry with kitchen paper, then peel the onions.

Preheat the barbecue. Thread the beetroot, onions and damp bay leaves onto the skewers, sprinkle with the olive oil and vinegar and season well with salt and pepper. Cook over medium hot coals for 20–25 minutes, turning occasionally, until charred and tender, then serve.

This is just the ticket for those who don't eat meat but love a good burger. The onion jam can be made in advance and kept in the refrigerator for several days.

mushroom burgers
with charred chilli mayonnaise

1 large fresh red chilli

½ recipe Mayonnaise (page 113)

2 tablespoons extra virgin olive oil

4 large portobello mushrooms, trimmed

4 burger buns, split in half

salad leaves

sea salt and freshly ground black pepper

onion jam

2 tablespoons olive oil

2 red onions, thinly sliced

4 tablespoons redcurrant jelly

1 tablespoon red wine vinegar

serves 4

To make the onion jam. Heat the olive oil in a saucepan, add the onions and fry gently for 15 minutes or until very soft. Add a pinch of salt, the redcurrant jelly, vinegar and 2 tablespoons water and cook for a further 15 minutes or until the mixture is glossy with a jam-like consistency. Remove from the heat and let cool.

Preheat the barbecue, then grill the chilli whole over hot coals for 1–2 minutes or until the skin is charred and blackened. Transfer to a plastic bag, seal and let cool slightly. Peel the chilli, then remove and discard the seeds. Chop the flesh and put into a food processor. Add the mayonnaise and process until the sauce is speckled red. Taste and adjust the seasoning, if necessary.

Brush the olive oil over the mushrooms, season well with salt and pepper and cook on the grill rack, stem side down, for 5 minutes. Flip and cook for a further 5 minutes until the mushrooms are tender.

Toast the burger bun halves for a few moments on the barbecue and fill with the mushrooms, salad leaves, onion jam and a spoonful of the chilli mayonnaise.

The nut sauce, tarator, served with these leeks is found in Middle Eastern cooking, though cooks there would use ground almonds or walnuts. If the sauce is made in advance, whisk well before use.

charred leeks with tarator sauce

750 g baby leeks, trimmed

2–3 tablespoons extra virgin olive oil

salt

a few lemon wedges, to serve

tarator sauce

50 g macadamia nuts, toasted

25 g fresh breadcrumbs

2 garlic cloves, crushed

100 ml extra virgin olive oil

1 tablespoon lemon juice

2 tablespoons boiling water

sea salt and freshly ground black pepper

serves 4

To make the sauce, put the nuts into a food processor and grind coarsely, then add the breadcrumbs, garlic, salt and pepper and process again to form a smooth paste. Transfer to a bowl and very gradually whisk in the olive oil, lemon juice and the 2 tablespoons boiling water to form a sauce. Season to taste with salt and pepper.

Preheat the barbecue. Brush the leeks with a little olive oil, season with salt and cook over medium hot coals for 6–10 minutes, turning occasionally, until charred and tender. Transfer to a serving plate, sprinkle with olive oil, then pour the sauce over the top and serve with the lemon wedges.

fish and seafood

Whole fish are ideally suited to grilling because the skin protects the delicate flesh. I usually slash the skin before marinating and cooking, because it helps the flesh to absorb the flavour of the marinade and also allows the fish to cook more evenly.

You can use a special fish basket, which will stop the fish sticking to the grill rack and make it easier to turn, but I find that as long as the rack is well oiled (page 11), this is not usually necessary.

Shellfish is also excellent cooked on the grill. Prawns, lobsters, crabs, clams and mussels are all delicious and need little to adorn them other than a wedge of lemon and a sprinkling of extra virgin olive oil. Cooking clams or mussels in a parcel is another great way to cook shellfish so all their delicious juices are retained (page 62).

salt-crusted prawns
with tomato, avocado and olive salad

Coating the prawns with sea salt protects the flesh during cooking so that when you shell them, the meat inside is sweet and moist.

20 large uncooked prawns

1 tablespoon extra virgin olive oil

3 tablespoons salt

tomato, avocado and olive salad

4–6 large ripe tomatoes, sliced

1 large ripe avocado, halved, stoned and sliced

50 g pitted black olives

a handful of fresh mint leaves

4 tablespoons extra virgin olive oil

1 tablespoon Reduced Balsamic Vinegar (page 30)

shavings of fresh Parmesan cheese

sea salt and freshly ground black pepper

to serve

lemon wedges

salad leaves

serves 4

To prepare the salad, put the tomatoes and avocado onto a plate with the olives and mint. Put the olive oil and vinegar into a jug and stir well, then sprinkle over the salad. Add the Parmesan and salt and pepper to taste.

Using kitchen scissors, cut down the back of each prawn to reveal the intestinal vein. Pull it out and discard. Wash the prawns under cold running water, pat dry with kitchen paper and put into a bowl. Add the olive oil and toss well. Put the salt onto a plate and use to coat the prawns.

Preheat the barbecue, then cook the prawns over hot coals for 2–3 minutes on each side until cooked through. Let cool slightly, peel off the shells and serve with lemon wedges and salad leaves.

Whole scallops grilled on the half shell look just great. If you can't find any with shells, don't despair, simply thread whole scallops onto soaked wooden skewers, brush with the melted butter mixture and grill for 1 minute on each side. Serve, sprinkled with the remaining butter and coriander.

scallops with lemongrass and lime butter

2 stalks of lemongrass

grated zest and juice of ½ large unwaxed lime

100 g butter, softened

1 small fresh red chilli, deseeded and finely chopped

1 tablespoon Thai fish sauce

24 scallops on the half shell

1 tablespoon chopped fresh coriander

freshly ground black pepper

serves 4

Using a sharp knife, trim the lemongrass stalks to about 15 cm, then remove the tough outer leaves. Chop the inner stalk very thinly and put into a saucepan with the lime zest and juice, butter, chilli and fish sauce. Heat gently until the butter has melted, then simmer for 1 minute. Remove from the heat and let cool.

Remove and discard the corals from the scallops and make sure the meat is not still attached to the shell. If it is, carefully cut through the muscle to release the scallop. Leave the scallops on the shells and spoon a little of the butter mixture over each one.

Preheat the barbecue, then put the shells on the grill rack and cook for 3–4 minutes, turning the scallops over half-way through with tongs. Serve at once sprinkled with chopped coriander and freshly ground black pepper.

This is a great way to cook clams on the barbecue, where all the wonderful juices are collected in the foil parcel. Mop them up with plenty of crusty bread.

clam parcels with garlic butter

1 kg vongole clams

125 g unsalted butter, softened

grated zest and juice of ½ unwaxed lemon

2 garlic cloves, crushed

2 tablespoons chopped fresh parsley

freshly ground black pepper

crusty bread, to serve

serves 4

Wash the clams under cold running water and scrub the shells. Discard any with broken shells or any that refuse to close when tapped lightly with a knife. Shake the clams dry and divide between 4 pieces of foil.

Put the butter, lemon zest and juice, garlic, parsley and pepper into a bowl and beat well, then divide equally between the clams. Wrap the foil over the clams and seal the edges to form parcels.

Preheat the barbecue, then put the parcels onto the grill rack and cook for 5 minutes. Check 1 parcel to see if the clams have opened and serve if ready or cook a little longer, if needed. Serve with crusty bread.

Smoking food on the barbecue is simply magical – the flavours are truly wonderful. You will need a barbecue with a lid for this recipe, and if you have a gas barbecue follow the instructions on page 11 for indirect grill-smoking.

hot-smoked **creole salmon**

4 salmon fillets, skinned, about 200 g each

1 recipe Creole Rub
(page 121)

a large handful of wood chips, such as hickory, soaked in cold water for 1 hour, drained

mango and sesame salsa

1 large ripe mango, peeled, stoned and chopped

4 spring onions, chopped

1 fresh red chilli, deseeded and chopped

1 garlic clove, crushed

1 tablespoon light soy sauce

1 tablespoon lime juice

1 teaspoon sesame oil

½ tablespoon sugar

1 tablespoon chopped fresh coriander

sea salt and freshly ground black pepper

serves 4

Wash the salmon under cold running water and pat dry with kitchen paper. Using a small pair of tweezers, pull out any bones, then put the fish into a dish and work the Creole Rub all over it. Let marinate in the refrigerator for at least 1 hour.

To make the salsa, put the chopped mango in a bowl, then add the spring onions, chilli, garlic, soy sauce, lime juice, sesame oil, sugar, coriander, salt and pepper. Mix well and set aside for 30 minutes to let the flavours infuse.

Preheat the charcoal grill for indirect grilling (page 11), put a drip tray in the middle and, when the coals are hot, tip half the soaked wood chips onto each pile. Cover with the lid, leaving any air vents open during cooking.

As soon as the wood chips start to smoke, put the salmon fillets into the centre of the grill, cover and cook for about 15–20 minutes or until the salmon is cooked through.

To test the fish, press the salmon with your finger, the flesh should feel firm and start to open into flakes. Serve hot or cold with the mango and sesame salsa.

Chunks of swordfish coated in a spicy rub, then barbecued on skewers and served with freshly cooked couscous, make the perfect lunch. Chicken would also work well, if you prefer.

moroccan fish skewers
with couscous

750 g swordfish steak

extra virgin olive oil

½ recipe Moroccan Rub (page 121)

24 large bay leaves, soaked in cold water for 1 hour

2 lemons, cut into 24 chunks

lemon juice

COUSCOUS

250 g couscous

300 ml boiling water

50 g freshly grated Parmesan cheese

50 g melted butter

1 tablespoon chopped fresh thyme

sea salt and freshly ground black pepper

8 bamboo skewers, soaked in cold water for 1 hour

serves 4

Using a sharp knife, cut the swordfish into 32 cubes and put into a shallow ceramic dish. Add a sprinkle of olive oil and the Moroccan Rub, toss well until the fish is evenly coated. Let marinate in the refrigerator for 1 hour.

About 10 minutes before cooking the fish, put the couscous into a sieve and rinse under cold running water to moisten all the grains, then put into a steamer and steam for 10 minutes or until the grains have softened. Transfer the couscous to a warmed serving dish and immediately stir in the Parmesan cheese, melted butter, thyme and seasonings. Keep the couscous warm.

Meanwhile, preheat the barbecue. Thread the fish, bay leaves and chunks of lemon onto the soaked bamboo skewers and cook over hot coals for 3–4 minutes, turning half-way through until cooked. Serve the skewers on a bed of couscous, sprinkled with olive oil and lemon juice.

Note One hour is sufficient to flavour the fish with the spice rub, any longer and the flavours of the rub can become overpowering.

Even if the snapper has already been scaled by the fishmonger, go over it again to remove any stray scales – they are huge! A fish grilling basket could also be used to cook this fish.

red snapper with parsley salad

4 red snapper, cleaned and well scaled, about 350 g each

1 recipe Herb, Lemon and Garlic Marinade (page 118)

parsley salad

50 g raisins

2 tablespoons verjuice or white grape juice

leaves from a large bunch of fresh parsley

25 g pine nuts, toasted

50 g feta cheese, crumbled

3 tablespoons extra virgin olive oil

2 teaspoons balsamic vinegar

sea salt and freshly ground black pepper

serves 4

Using a sharp knife, cut several slashes into each side of the fish. Put into a shallow ceramic dish and add the marinade. Let marinate in the refrigerator for 4 hours, but return to room temperature for 1 hour before cooking.

Just before cooking the fish, make the salad. Put the raisins into a bowl, add the verjuice and let soak for 15 minutes. Drain and set the liquid aside. Put the parsley, pine nuts, soaked raisins and feta into a bowl. Put the olive oil, vinegar and reserved raisin liquid into a separate bowl and mix well. Pour over the salad and toss until the leaves are well coated. Season with salt and pepper.

Preheat the barbecue, then cook the fish over hot coals for 4–5 minutes on each side, let rest briefly and serve at once with the parsley salad.

Note Verjuice, which is used in the salad dressing, is produced from the juice of unripe grapes. It is available from Italian delicatessens. If you can't find it, use white grape juice instead.

Dukkah is a Middle Eastern dish comprising mixed nuts and spices, which are ground to a coarse powder and served as a dip for warm bread. Here, it is used as a coating for grilled tuna. Preserved lemons are available from good delicatessens and Middle Eastern food stores.

dukkah crusted tuna
with preserved lemon salsa

4 tuna steaks, about
200 g each

3 tablespoons sesame seeds

2 tablespoons coriander seeds

½ tablespoon cumin seeds

25 g blanched
almonds, chopped

½ teaspoon salt

freshly ground black pepper

olive oil, for brushing

preserved lemon salsa

25 g preserved lemons

25 g semi-dried tomatoes

2 spring onions, very
finely chopped

1 tablespoon coarsely
chopped fresh parsley

3 tablespoons extra virgin
olive oil

¼ teaspoon caster sugar

serves 4

To make the salsa, chop the preserved lemon and tomatoes finely and put into a bowl. Stir in the spring onions, parsley, olive oil and sugar and set aside until ready to serve.

Wash the tuna steaks under cold running water and pat dry with kitchen paper.

Put the sesame seeds into a dry frying pan and toast over medium heat until golden and aromatic. Remove and let cool. Repeat with the coriander seeds, cumin seeds and almonds. Transfer to a spice grinder (or clean coffee grinder) and grind roughly. Alternatively, use a mortar and pestle. Add the salt and a little pepper.

Preheat the barbecue. Brush the tuna steaks with olive oil and coat with the dukkah mixture. Cook over hot coals for 1 minute on each side, top with the salsa and serve.

meat and poultry

Be it a juicy steak or homely sausages, meat and the grill are a match made in heaven. The wonderful flavour of the charred exterior combined with a smoky and succulent interior is very hard to beat.

When testing the recipes in this book, I was surprised just how many different cuts of meat and poultry could be grilled with such success. From a simple (but none the less wonderful) hot dog to a whole chicken, from the perfect steak to tea-smoked duck – everything was memorable.

Using marinades and rubs to flavour and tenderize the food is great with meat and poultry – and good for the cook too, because this part can be done in advance or even overnight. Then it's barbecue time and you can throw it on the 'barbie', step back and relax in the knowledge that in a few minutes you will have created wonderful food, full of flavour.

The fact that there never seems to be as much washing up to do afterwards is, of course, an added bonus.

This delicious concoction of olives, lemons, fresh marjoram and succulent chicken makes an ideal main course for a barbecue party. Serve with a selection of salads, such as tomato and basil.

olive-infused chicken
with charred lemons

1.5 kg chicken

75 g pitted black olives

4 tablespoons extra virgin olive oil

1 teaspoon salt

2 tablespoons chopped fresh marjoram

freshly squeezed juice of 1 lemon plus 2 lemons, halved

freshly ground black pepper

serves 4

To prepare the chicken, put it onto a board with the back facing upwards and, using kitchen scissors, cut along each side of the backbone and remove it completely. Using your fingers, gently ease the skin away from the flesh, taking care not to tear the skin, then put the chicken into a large, shallow dish. Put the olives, olive oil, salt, marjoram and lemon juice into a separate bowl and mix well, then pour over the chicken and push as many of the olives as possible up between the skin and flesh of the chicken. Let marinate in the refrigerator for 2 hours.

Preheat the barbecue, then cook the chicken cut side down over medium hot coals for 15 minutes. Using tongs, turn the chicken over and cook for a further 10 minutes until the skin is charred, the flesh is cooked through and the juices run clear when the thickest part of the meat is pierced with a skewer. While the chicken is cooking, add the halved lemons to the grill and cook for about 10–15 minutes until charred and tender on all sides.

Let the chicken rest for 10 minutes before cutting into 4 pieces and serving with the lemons.

Cooking with the lid on your barbecue creates the same effect as cooking in a conventional oven. If you don't have a barbecue with a lid, you can cut the chicken in half and cook on the grill for about 15 minutes on each side.

whole chicken
roasted on the barbecue

1.5 kg chicken

1 lemon, halved

4 garlic cloves, peeled

a small bunch of fresh thyme

extra virgin olive oil

sea salt and freshly ground black pepper

serves 4–6

Wash the chicken thoroughly under cold running water and pat dry with kitchen paper.

Rub the chicken all over with the halved lemon, then put the lemon halves inside the body cavity with the garlic cloves and thyme. Rub a little olive oil into the skin and season liberally with salt and pepper.

Preheat the barbecue for indirect grilling (page 11) and put a drip tray in the middle. Brush the grill rack with oil and put the chicken above the drip tray. Cover with the lid, then cook over medium hot coals for 1 hour or until the skin is golden, the flesh is cooked through and the juices run clear when the thickest part of the meat is pierced with a skewer. If any bloody juices appear, then cook a little longer.

Let the chicken rest for 10 minutes before serving.

This spice dip, called zahtar, is served with pita bread. It is sold ready-made from Middle Eastern stores, but it is very easy to make your own.

chicken skewers
with thyme and sesame dip

3 tablespoons zahtar spice mix (below)

3 tablespoons extra virgin olive oil

750 g boneless chicken breast fillets

zahtar spice mix

3 tablespoons sesame seeds, toasted

30 g fresh thyme leaves

½ teaspoon salt

to serve

chilli oil

1–2 lemons, cut into wedges

mixed salad leaves

8 wooden skewers soaked in cold water for 30 minutes

serves 4

To make the zahtar spice mix, put the sesame seeds into a dry frying pan and toast over medium heat until golden and aromatic. Remove, let cool, then transfer to a spice grinder (or clean coffee grinder). Add the thyme and salt, then blend to a coarse powder. Alternatively, use a mortar and pestle. You will need 3 tablespoons for this recipe (put the remainder into an airtight container and keep in a cool place for future use).

Put the 3 tablespoons of zahtar spice mix and olive oil into a shallow dish and mix well. Cut the chicken into bite-sized pieces, add to the zahtar oil and toss well until coated. Let marinate in the refrigerator for at least 2 hours.

Preheat the barbecue, then thread the chicken pieces onto the soaked wooden skewers and cook over hot coals for 2–3 minutes on each side. Remove from the heat, let rest briefly, sprinkle with chilli oil and lemon juice and serve hot with salad leaves.

The tea-smoke mixture adds a lovely spicy aroma to the duck. I like to cook the duck with the skin on, but this can be removed after cooking, if preferred. You will need a barbecue with a lid. If you have a gas barbecue follow the instructions on page 11 for indirect grilling and smoking.

tea-smoked asian spiced
duck breast

4 duck breast fillets, about 200 g each

1 recipe Thai Spice Marinade (page 118)

tea-smoke mixture

8 tablespoons soft brown sugar

8 tablespoons long grain rice

8 tablespoons tea leaves

2 cinnamon sticks, bruised

1 star anise

to serve

Mango and Sesame Salsa (page 65, 110)

Asian salad leaves

serves 4

Using a sharp knife, cut several slashes into the duck skin, then put the duck into a shallow dish. Add the marinade, cover and let marinate in the refrigerator overnight. Remove from the refrigerator 1 hour before cooking.

Preheat the barbecue for indirect grilling (page 11) and put a foil drip tray in the middle.

Put all the ingredients for the smoke mixture into a bowl and mix well. Transfer to a sheet of foil, fold the edges over and around the smoke mixture, seal well, then pierce the foil in about 10 places.

Put the foil parcel directly on top of the hot coals, cover with the barbecue lid and wait until smoke appears. Remove the duck from the marinade and put onto the grill rack over the drip tray, cover and cook for 15 minutes until cooked through. Discard the marinade.

Let the duck rest briefly, then serve with the mango and sesame salsa and salad leaves.

This hot dog recipe calls for good-quality pork sausages rather than the more typical frankfurters usually associated with hot dogs. I think this version tastes better, especially with the caramelized onions and wholegrain mustard.

top dogs

2 onions, cut into thin wedges

2–3 tablespoons extra virgin olive oil

1 tablespoon chopped fresh sage

4 good-quality pork sausages, pricked

4 hot dog rolls

4 tablespoons wholegrain mustard

2 ripe tomatoes, sliced

sea salt and freshly ground black pepper

Barbecue Sauce (page 116), to serve (optional)

serves 4

Put the onion wedges into a bowl, add the olive oil, sage and a little salt and pepper and mix well. Preheat the flat plate on the gas barbecue and cook the onions for 15–20 minutes, stirring occasionally until golden and tender. If you have a charcoal barbecue, cook the onions in a frying pan on top of the stove or on the barbecue. Keep hot.

Meanwhile, cook the sausages over hot coals for 10–12 minutes, turning frequently until charred and cooked through. Transfer to a plate and let rest briefly.

Cut the rolls almost in half, then put onto the grill rack and toast for a few minutes. Remove from the heat and spread with mustard. Fill with the tomatoes, sausages and onions. Add a little Barbecue Sauce, if using, and serve.

pork bangers

Everyone seems to enjoy sausages, and these homemade ones will be no exception. Made from pork, bacon and fresh sage, they are a delicious combination. Cook the sausages until browned all over and make sure that they are completely cooked through before serving.

25 g sausage skins*

375 g boneless pork shoulder, chopped

375 g pork belly, chopped

250 g smoked bacon, chopped

4 garlic cloves

4 tablespoons chopped fresh sage

1 tablespoon coarsely crushed black peppercorns

½ teaspoon freshly grated nutmeg

2 teaspoons salt

English or French mustard, to serve

serves 4

Put the sausage skins into a bowl of cold water and let soak for 2 hours. Rinse thoroughly, under cold running water, drain and pat dry with kitchen paper.

Working in batches, put the pork shoulder, pork belly and bacon into a food processor and mince coarsely. Alternatively, use a sharp knife to chop the meat very finely. Transfer to a bowl and stir in the garlic, sage, pepper, nutmeg and salt.

Spoon the filling into a piping bag fitted with a large plain nozzle. Slip the sausage skin over the nozzle and hold firmly in place with one hand. Squeeze in the sausage mixture, twisting into suitable lengths as you go to make 12 sausages.

Preheat the barbecue, then cook the sausages over hot coals for about 10 minutes, turning frequently until browned and cooked through. Serve hot with the mustard.

*Note You can buy sausage skins from most good butchers.

These grilled ribs are spicy, smoky, sticky, tender and lip-smackingly good. They may take a little time to prepare because of soaking and marinating, but they are simple to cook and definitely well worth the effort.

smoky barbecue ribs

2 racks pork spare ribs, about 650 g each

300 ml white wine vinegar

2 tablespoons soft brown sugar

1 tablespoon salt

1 tablespoon sweet paprika

2 teaspoons crushed black pepper

2 teaspoons onion powder

1 teaspoon garlic powder

¼ teaspoon cayenne pepper

150 ml Barbecue Sauce (page 116)

Cramy Coleslaw (page 113), to serve

serves 4

Wash the ribs under cold running water and pat dry with kitchen paper. Put the ribs into a large dish, add the vinegar and let soak for 4 hours or overnight. Rinse the ribs well and pat dry with kitchen paper.

Put the sugar, salt, paprika, pepper, onion powder, garlic powder and cayenne into a bowl and mix well. Rub the mixture all over the ribs and let marinate in the refrigerator for 2 hours.

Preheat the barbecue, then cook the ribs over low heat for 20 minutes on each side. Brush with the barbecue sauce and cook for a further 15 minutes on each side until the ribs are lightly charred, tender and sticky. Remove and let cool briefly before serving with Coleslaw.

Although pork should not be served rare it is quite easy to overcook it, leaving the meat dry and tough. A good test is to pierce the meat with a skewer, leave it there for a second, remove it and carefully feel how hot it is – it should feel warm, not too hot or too cold, for the perfect result.

sage-rubbed **pork chops**

2 tablespoons chopped fresh sage

2 tablespoons wholegrain mustard

2 tablespoons extra virgin olive oil

4 large pork chops

sea salt and freshly ground black pepper

1 recipe Smoky Tomato Salsa (page 111), to serve

serves 4

Put the sage, mustard and olive oil into a bowl and mix well. Season with a little salt and pepper, then spread the mixture all over the chops. Let marinate in the refrigerator for 1 hour.

Preheat the barbecue, then cook the chops over hot coals for 2½–3 minutes on each side until browned and cooked through. Serve hot with the smoky tomato salsa.

Like many Vietnamese dishes these delicious pork balls are served wrapped in a lettuce leaf with plenty of fresh herbs and Sweet Chilli Sauce.

vietnamese pork balls

1 stalk of lemongrass

500 g minced pork

125 g pork belly, minced

25 g breadcrumbs

6 kaffir lime leaves, very finely sliced

2 garlic cloves, crushed

2 cm fresh ginger, grated

1 fresh red chilli, deseeded and chopped

2 tablespoons Thai fish sauce

to serve

lettuce leaves

a handful of fresh herb leaves, such as mint, coriander and Thai basil

Sweet Chilli Sauce (page 116)

4 wooden skewers soaked in cold water for 30 minutes

serves 4

Using a sharp knife, trim the lemongrass stalks to about 15 cm, then remove and discard the tough outer leaves. Chop the inner stalk very finely.

Put the minced pork and pork belly and breadcrumbs into a bowl, then add the lemongrass, lime leaves, garlic, ginger, chilli and fish sauce and mix well. Let marinate in the refrigerator for at least 1 hour.

Using your hands, shape the mixture into 20 small balls and carefully thread 5 onto each of the soaked wooden skewers. Preheat the barbecue, then brush the grill rack with oil. Cook the skewers over hot coals for 5–6 minutes, turning half-way through until cooked.

Serve the pork balls wrapped in the lettuce leaves with the herbs and sweet chilli sauce.

A good burger should be thick, moist, tender and juicy. These lamb burgers are all that and more. Serve in crusty rolls with a few slices of tomato, plenty of fresh salad leaves and a generous spoonful of the cool minty yoghurt dressing. The perfect burger for a barbecue party.

lamb burgers with mint yoghurt

650 g boneless lamb shoulder, cut into 2 cm cubes

100 g pork belly, chopped

1 onion, very finely chopped

2 garlic cloves, crushed

2 tablespoon ground cumin

2 teaspoons ground cinnamon

1 tablespoon dried oregano

2 teaspoons salt

50 g fresh breadcrumbs

1 tablespoon capers, drained and chopped

freshly ground black pepper

1 large free-range egg, beaten

mint yoghurt

200 g thick yoghurt

2 tablespoons chopped fresh mint

sea salt and freshly ground black pepper

to serve

4 crusty rolls

salad leaves

tomato slices

Put the lamb and pork into a food processor and process briefly until coarsely ground. Transfer to a bowl and, using your hands, work in the chopped onion, garlic, cumin, cinnamon, oregano, salt, breadcrumbs, capers, pepper and beaten egg. Cover and marinate in the refrigerator for at least 2 hours.

Put the yoghurt into a bowl and stir in the mint, then add a little salt and pepper to taste. Set aside until required.

Using damp hands, shape the meat into 8 burgers. Preheat the barbecue, then brush the grill rack with oil. Cook the burgers for about 3 minutes on each side.

Split the rolls in half and fill with the cooked burgers, salad leaves, tomato slices and a spoonful of mint yoghurt.

Variation

For a traditional hamburger, replace the lamb with beef, omit the spices and, instead of the capers, add 4 chopped anchovy fillets. Serve in burger buns with salad.

serves 4

Choosing the right steak for barbecue cooking is the first step to producing the perfect steak. There are several cuts you can use, such as fillet, T-bone or sirloin, but my own favourite is rib eye steak. As the name suggests, it is the 'eye' of the rib roast and is marbled with fat, giving a moist result. It has a good flavour and is not too huge.

rib eye steak with anchovy butter

125 g butter, softened

8 anchovy fillets in oil, drained and chopped coarsely

2 tablespoons chopped fresh parsley

4 rib eye steaks, about 250 g each

sea salt and freshly ground black pepper

serves 4

Put the butter, anchovies, parsley and a little pepper into a bowl and beat well. Transfer to a sheet of foil and roll up into a log. Chill until required.

Preheat the barbecue to high and brush the grill rack with oil. Season the steaks with salt and pepper and cook for 3 minutes on each side for rare, 4–5 minutes for medium and about 5–6 minutes for well done.

Transfer the steaks to a warmed serving plate and put 2 slices of anchovy butter on each one. Let rest for about 5 minutes before serving in order to set the juices.

If you can find porcini mushrooms all the better, but any field mushrooms will taste great cooked on the barbecue.

whole beef fillet
with mushrooms

500 g fillet of beef

1 tablespoon extra virgin olive oil, plus extra for brushing

1 tablespoon crushed black peppercorns

8 large porcini or portobello mushrooms

sea salt and freshly ground black pepper

Beetroot and Baby Onion Brochettes (page 50), to serve (optional)

dressing

100 ml extra virgin olive oil

1 garlic clove, chopped

1 tablespoon chopped fresh parsley

a squeeze of lemon juice

serves 4

Brush the beef with olive oil, press the peppercorns into the meat, then sprinkle with salt.

Preheat the barbecue to high, then cook the meat for 25 minutes, turning every 5 minutes or so until evenly browned on all sides. Cook the beef for 15 minutes for rare, 20 minutes for medium and 25 minutes for well done. Transfer the beef to a roasting tin, cover with foil and let rest for 10 minutes.

Brush the mushrooms with olive oil, season with salt and pepper, then put stem side down on the grill rack and cook for 5 minutes on each side. Transfer the mushrooms to the roasting tin and let rest for a further 1–2 minutes.

Meanwhile, put all the dressing ingredients into a bowl and mix well. Serve the beef in thick slices with the mushrooms, a sprinkle of the dressing and the Beetroot and Baby Onion Brochettes, if using.

This is probably the best way to cook lamb on the barbecue – the bone is removed and the meat opened out flat so it can cook quickly and evenly over the coals. If you don't fancy boning the lamb yourself, ask the butcher to do it for you.

butterflied lamb
with white bean salad

1.5–2 kg leg of lamb, butterflied

1 recipe Herb, Lemon and Garlic Marinade (page 118)

white bean salad

1 large red onion, finely chopped

3 cans haricot beans, about 400 g each, drained

2 garlic cloves, chopped

3 tomatoes, deseeded and chopped

75 ml extra virgin olive oil

1½ tablespoons red wine vinegar

2 tablespoons chopped fresh parsley

sea salt and freshly ground black pepper

1 recipe Salsa Verde (page 111), to serve

serves 8

To make the salad, put the onion into a colander, sprinkle with salt and let drain over a bowl for 30 minutes. Wash the onion under cold running water and dry well. Transfer to a bowl, then add the beans, garlic, tomatoes, olive oil, vinegar, parsley and salt and pepper to taste.

Put the lamb into a shallow dish, pour over the marinade, cover and let marinate in the refrigerator overnight. Remove from the refrigerator 1 hour before cooking.

Preheat the barbecue. Drain the lamb and discard the marinade. Cook over medium hot coals for 12–15 minutes on each side until charred on the outside but still pink in the middle (cook for a little longer if you prefer the meat less rare). Let the lamb rest for 10 minutes.

Cut the lamb into slices and serve with the White Bean Salad and Salsa Verde.

Serve this with the Courgette, Feta and Mint Salad (page 34) for a splendid Middle Eastern feast. Pieces of tender lamb, marinated in mint and yoghurt complement the warm chickpeas perfectly.

lamb kebabs with warm chickpea salad

750 g lamb fillet or boneless leg of lamb

1 recipe Minted Yoghurt Marinade (page 118)

warm chickpea salad

150 g dried chickpeas, soaked overnight in cold water, drained and rinsed

1 bay leaf

½ onion

6 tablespoons extra virgin olive oil, plus extra to serve

1 garlic clove, finely chopped

freshly squeezed juice of ½ lemon

a handful of fresh parsley leaves

a pinch of sweet paprika

sea salt and freshly ground black pepper

4 metal skewers

serves 4

Using a sharp knife, cut the lamb fillet into bite-sized pieces and put into a shallow dish. Add the marinade and stir well to coat the lamb. Let marinate in the refrigerator for 2–4 hours. Thread onto the skewers.

Prepare the chickpea salad 1 hour before barbecuing. Put the soaked chickpeas, bay leaf and onion into a heavy-based saucepan and cover with cold water. Bring to the boil and simmer for 45 minutes or until the chickpeas are tender, skimming off the foam from time to time.

Drain the chickpeas and transfer to a bowl. Remove the onion and bay leaf. Mash coarsely with a fork. Stir in the olive oil, garlic, lemon juice, parsley, paprika and salt and pepper to taste.

Meanwhile, preheat the barbecue, then cook the kebabs over hot coals for 6–8 minutes, turning half-way through until tender. Serve the kebabs on a bed of chickpea salad, sprinkled with a little extra olive oil.

accompaniments

I thought very hard about exactly what I wanted to put in this chapter. Should I just suggest a handful of recipes that work well with barbecued foods but can be cooked in the kitchen, or was it best to stick to the grill? In the end I decided on both.

First, if you are firing up the barbecue to cook the main course, utilize it while you can. This book explores the versatility of the barbecue, and grilling dishes like bread and polenta adds an extra dimension to the range of possibilities.

Second, to offer the reader as much variation as possible, I wanted to include a few great-tasting accompaniments. They are, after all, an essential part of a good barbecue and delicious classics like salsa or mayonnaise provide the perfect partners to almost all kinds of barbecued food. You'll also find examples given with the recipes in other chapters.

Grilled polenta triangles make a lovely accompaniment for grilled meats and fish or they can be used as a bruschetta-type base for grilled vegetables, such as Vegetable Antipasti (page 27).

grilled polenta

2 teaspoons salt

175 g instant polenta

2 garlic clove, crushed

1 tablespoon chopped fresh basil

50 g butter

50 g freshly grated Parmesan cheese

freshly ground black pepper

olive oil, for brushing

a rectangular cake tin, 23 x 30 cm, greased

serves 8

Pour 1 litre water into a heavy-based saucepan and bring to the boil. Add the salt and gradually whisk in the polenta in a steady stream, using a large, metal whisk.

Cook over low heat, stirring constantly with a wooden spoon for 5 minutes or until the grains have swelled and thickened.

Remove the saucepan from the heat and immediately beat in the garlic, basil, butter and Parmesan until the mixture is smooth. Pour into the greased tin and let cool completely.

Preheat the barbecue. Turn out the polenta onto a board and cut into large squares, then cut in half again to form triangles. Brush the triangles with a little olive oil and cook over hot coals for 2–3 minutes on each side until charred and heated through.

Hot from the grill, this aromatic herb bread is delicious used to mop up the wonderful meat juices, or eaten on its own with olive oil for dipping.

grilled rosemary flatbread

250 g strong white flour, plus extra for dusting

1½ teaspoons fast-acting yeast

1 teaspoon salt

1 tablespoon chopped fresh rosemary

120 ml hot water

2 tablespoons extra virgin olive oil, plus extra for brushing

serves 4

Sift the flour into the bowl of an electric mixer and stir in the yeast, salt and rosemary. Add the hot water and olive oil and knead with the dough hook at high speed for about 8 minutes or until the dough is smooth and elastic. Alternatively, sift the flour into a large bowl and stir in the yeast, salt and rosemary. Make a well in the centre, then add the hot water and olive oil and mix to form a soft dough. Turn out onto a lightly floured work surface and knead until the dough is smooth and elastic.

Shape the dough into a ball, then put into an oiled bowl, cover with a tea towel and let rise in a warm place for 45–60 minutes or until doubled in size.

Punch down the dough and divide into quarters. Roll each piece out on a lightly floured work surface to make a 15 cm long oval.

Preheat the barbecue to low. Brush the bread with a little olive oil and cook for 5 minutes, then brush the top with the remaining olive oil, flip and cook for a further 4–5 minutes until the bread is cooked through. Serve hot.

This is a fun version of garlic bread, and the slightly smoky flavour you get from the coals is delicious. You can also add cubes of cheese such as mozzarella or fontina to the skewers.

garlic bread skewers

1 baguette

150 ml extra virgin olive oil

2 garlic cloves, crushed

2 tablespoons chopped fresh parsley

sea salt and freshly ground black pepper

6–8 wooden skewers soaked in cold water for 30 minutes

serves 6–8

Cut the bread into 2 cm thick slices, then cut the slices crossways to make half moons.

Put the olive oil, garlic, parsley, salt and pepper into a large bowl, add the bread and toss until well coated with the parsley and oil.

Preheat the barbecue. Thread the garlic bread onto skewers and cook over medium hot coals for 2–3 minutes on each side until toasted.

Variation

Cut 250 g mozzarella cheese into about 24 small pieces. Thread a piece of bread onto the skewer and continue to alternate the cheese and bread. Cook as in the main recipe.

salsas

mango and sesame salsa

This tangy salsa makes a wonderful accompaniment to all types of grilled meats and fish. I particularly like it with salmon or ocean trout. If mango is unavailable, use other fruits such as papaya, pineapple or even peaches.

1 large ripe mango
4 spring onions, trimmed and finely chopped
1 small red chilli, deseeded and chopped
1 garlic clove, crushed
1 tablespoon light soy sauce
1 tablespoon lime juice
1 teaspoon sesame oil
½ tablespoon caster sugar
1 tablespoon chopped fresh coriander
sea salt and freshly ground black pepper

makes about 200 ml

Peel the mango and cut the flesh away from the pit. Cut the flesh into cubes and mix with all the remaining ingredients and season to taste.

Set aside for 30 minutes for the flavours to infuse before serving.

salsa verde

This Italian green herb sauce is enhanced with the piquant flavours of capers and green olives. It goes particularly well with grilled lamb or chicken.

a bunch of parsley leaves (about 25 g)

a small bunch of mixed fresh herbs such as basil, chives and mint

1 garlic clove, chopped

1 tablespoon pitted green olives

1 tablespoon capers, drained and washed

2 anchovy fillets, washed and chopped

1 teaspoon Dijon mustard

2 teaspoons white wine vinegar

150 ml extra virgin olive oil

salt and pepper

makes about 200 ml

Put all the ingredients except the oil into the food processor and blend to a smooth paste. Gradually pour in the oil to form a sauce, then taste and adjust the seasonings. The salsa may be stored in the refrigerator for up to 3 days.

smoky tomato salsa

Barbecuing the tomatoes, chillies, garlic and onion enhances their flavours, giving a delicate smoky quality. Serve with burgers, grilled meat, or fish, or spread on bruschetta.

4 ripe plum tomatoes

2 large fresh red chillies

4 whole garlic cloves, peeled

1 red onion, quartered

4 tablespoons extra virgin olive oil

1 tablespoon lemon juice

2 tablespoons chopped fresh coriander

sea salt and freshly ground black pepper

2 wooden skewers, soaked in cold water for 30 minutes

makes about 500 ml

Using tongs, hold the tomatoes over the flames of the barbecue for about 1 minute, turning frequently, until the skin is charred all over. Let cool, peel, cut in half and remove and discard the seeds, then chop the flesh. Repeat with the chillies.

Thread the garlic cloves and onion wedges onto separate skewers. Cook the garlic over hot coals for 10–12 minutes until they are charred and softened. Let cool, remove from the skewers and cut into cubes.

Put the tomato, chilli, garlic and onion into a bowl and stir in the olive oil, lemon juice and coriander. Season to taste with salt and pepper and use as required. Alternatively, spoon the salsa into sterilized jars and seal tightly. Store in the refrigerator until ready to use.

mayonnaise

2 egg yolks

2 teaspoons white wine vinegar or lemon juice

2 teaspoons Dijon mustard

¼ teaspoon salt

300 ml olive oil

freshly ground black pepper

makes about 300 ml

Put the egg yolks, vinegar, mustard and salt into a food processor and blend briefly until frothy. With the machine running, gradually pour in the olive oil in a slow steady stream until all the oil is incorporated and the sauce is thick and glossy.

If the sauce is too thick, add 1–2 tablespoons boiling water and blend again briefly. Season to taste with salt and pepper, then cover the surface of the mayonnaise with clingfilm. Store in the refrigerator for up to 3 days.

Note I prefer not to use an extra virgin olive oil when making mayonnaise because I find the sauce can become slightly bitter. As an alternative, I use regular olive oil or, when I can find it, a French extra virgin olive oil, which tends to be milder than others.

creamy coleslaw

250 g white cabbage, thinly sliced

175 g carrots, grated

½ white onion, thinly sliced

1 teaspoon salt

2 teaspoons caster sugar

1 tablespoon white wine vinegar

50 g Mayonnaise (left)

2 tablespoons double cream

1 tablespoon wholegrain mustard

sea salt and freshly ground black pepper

serves 4

Put the cabbage, carrots and onion into a colander and sprinkle with the salt, sugar and vinegar. Stir well and let drain over a bowl for 30 minutes.

Squeeze out excess liquid from the vegetables and put into a large bowl. Put the mayonnaise, cream and mustard into a separate bowl and mix well, then stir into the cabbage mixture. Season to taste with salt and pepper and serve. Store in the refrigerator for up to 3 days.

basics

With all methods of cooking, there are certain dishes that people use time and time again, such as a marinade, sauce or rub, so I have put all these in one chapter for convenience.

Marinades and rubs enhance the flavour of the food, but the main difference is that a marinade can be discarded while a rub is retained throughout the cooking process. This results in a more highly flavoured meat. If the food is to be removed from the marinade before cooking, it is important to leave it long enough to absorb all those wonderful flavours. If you have time, marinate the day before so the flavours can really penetrate properly. When using a marinade or a rub I find it really useful to use a Zip-lock bag, so you can turn the ingredients several times to distribute the flavours evenly.

No barbecue would be complete without those delicious sauces that accompany char-grilled meat and fish. The most famous of them all is the barbecue sauce which you will find in hundreds of guises. I have included two – a classic American sauce, ideal for ribs, and a spicy Asian-style sauce.

sauces

barbecue sauce

200 ml tomato passata

100 ml maple syrup

50 ml dark treacle

50 ml tomato ketchup

50 ml white wine vinegar

3 tablespoons Worcestershire sauce

1 tablespoon Dijon mustard

1 teaspoon garlic powder

¼ teaspoon hot paprika

sea salt and freshly ground black pepper

makes about 400 ml

Put all the ingredients into a small saucepan, bring to the boil and simmer gently for 10–15 minutes until reduced slightly and thickened. Season to taste with salt and pepper and let cool.

Pour into an airtight container and store in the refrigerator for up to 2 weeks.

sweet chilli sauce

6 large red chillies, deseeded and chopped

4 garlic cloves, chopped

1 teaspoon grated fresh ginger

1 teaspoon salt

100 ml rice wine vinegar

100 g sugar

makes about 200 ml

Put the chillies, garlic, ginger and salt into a food processor and blend to a coarse paste. Transfer to a saucepan, add the vinegar and sugar, bring to the boil and simmer gently, part-covered, for 5 minutes until the mixture becomes a thin syrup. Remove from the heat and let cool.

Pour into an airtight container and store in the refrigerator for up to 2 weeks.

asian barbecue sauce

100 ml tomato passata

50 ml hoisin sauce

1 teaspoon hot chilli sauce

2 garlic cloves, crushed

2 tablespoons sweet soy sauce

1 tablespoon rice wine vinegar

1 teaspoon ground coriander

½ teaspoon ground cinnamon

¼ teaspoon Chinese five-spice pepper

makes about 350 ml

Put all the ingredients into a small saucepan, add 100 ml water, bring to the boil and simmer gently for 10 minutes. Remove from the heat and let cool.

Pour into an airtight container and store in the refrigerator for up to 2 weeks.

Note The recipe for Reduced Balsamic Vinegar (far right) is given on page 30.

marinades

herb, lemon and garlic marinade

2 sprigs of rosemary

2 sprigs of thyme

4 bay leaves

2 large garlic cloves, coarsely chopped

pared zest of 1 unwaxed lemon

1 teaspoon black peppercorns, coarsely crushed

200 ml extra virgin olive oil

makes about 300 ml

Strip the rosemary and thyme leaves from the stalk and put into a mortar. Add the bay leaves, garlic and lemon zest and pound with a pestle to release the aromas.

Put the mixture into a bowl and add the peppercorns and olive oil. Set aside to infuse until ready to use.

thai spice marinade

2 stalks of lemongrass

6 kaffir lime leaves

2 garlic cloves, coarsely chopped

2 cm fresh ginger, coarsely chopped

4 coriander roots, washed and dried

2 small fresh red chillies, deseeded and coarsely chopped

200 ml extra virgin olive oil

2 tablespoons sesame oil

2 tablespoons Thai fish sauce

makes about 300 ml

Using a sharp knife, trim the lemongrass stalk to 15 cm, then remove and discard the tough outer layers. Chop the inner stalk coarsely.

Put the lemongrass stalks, lime leaves, garlic, ginger, coriander roots and chillies into a mortar and pound with a pestle to release the aromas.

Put the mixture into a bowl, add the oils and fish sauce and set aside to infuse until ready to use.

minted yoghurt marinade

2 teaspoons coriander seeds

1 teaspoon cumin seeds

250 ml thick yoghurt

juice of ½ lemon

1 tablespoon extra virgin olive oil

2 garlic cloves, crushed

1 teaspoon grated fresh ginger

½ teaspoon salt

2 tablespoons chopped fresh mint

¼ teaspoon chilli powder

makes about 275 ml

Put the spices into a dry frying pan and toast over medium heat until golden and aromatic. Remove from the heat and let cool. Transfer to a spice grinder (or clean coffee grinder) and crush to a coarse powder. Alternatively, use a mortar and pestle.

Put the spices into a bowl, add the yoghurt, lemon juice, garlic, ginger, salt, mint and chilli powder and mix well. Set aside to infuse until ready to use.

rubs

creole rub

½ small onion, finely chopped

1 garlic clove, finely chopped

1 tablespoon chopped fresh thyme

1 tablespoon paprika

1 teaspoon ground cumin

1 teaspoon table salt

¼ teaspoon cayenne pepper

1 tablespoon brown sugar

a little freshly ground black pepper

makes about 6 tablespoons

Put all the ingredients into a small bowl, stir well and set aside to infuse until ready to use.

moroccan rub

1 tablespoon coriander seeds

1 teaspoon cumin seeds

2 cinnamon sticks

1 teaspoon whole allspice berries

6 cloves

a pinch of saffron threads

1 teaspoon ground turmeric

2 teaspoons dried onion flakes

1 teaspoon salt

½ teaspoon paprika

makes about 6 tablespoons

Put the whole spices and saffron threads into a dry frying pan and toast over medium heat for about 1–2 minutes or until golden and aromatic. Remove from the heat and let cool. Transfer to a spice grinder (or clean coffee grinder) and crush to a coarse powder. Alternatively, use a mortar and pestle.

Put the spices into a bowl, add the remaining ingredients and mix well. Set aside to infuse until ready to use.

fragrant asian rub

4 whole star anise

2 teaspoons Szechuan peppercorns

1 teaspoon fennel seeds

2 small pieces of cassia bark or 1 cinnamon stick, broken

6 cloves

2 garlic cloves, finely chopped

grated zest of 2 unwaxed limes

1 teaspoon salt

makes about 6 tablespoons

Put the whole spices into a dry frying pan and toast over medium heat for 1–2 minutes or until golden and aromatic. Remove from the heat and let cool. Transfer to a spice grinder (or clean coffee mill) and crush to a coarse powder. Alternatively, use a mortar and pestle.

Put the spices into a bowl, add the garlic, lime zest and salt and mix well. Set aside to infuse until ready to use.

sweet things and drinks

This chapter was such fun to write and test. The puddings were delicious and our friends ignored their waistlines for the duration. Many fruits are ideally suited to grilling, which brings out their natural sweet flavour. Bananas and pineapples are suitable as well as firmer fruits, such as pears, figs or plums. However, if you are cooking softer fruits or berries, wrap them in a foil parcel to retain all the lovely juices (page 128).

Of course devising the drinks was the best fun of all. It's great to offer a selection of both alcoholic and non-alcoholic drinks at a barbecue – people bring their children to these parties, and someone always has to drive, so I have tried to include drinks for everyone. Long, cool refreshing drinks such as the Strawberry, Pear and Orange Frappé and drinks based on Ginger and Lime Cordial (both page 136) are perfect for the abstainers and children. For the others, summery drinks like Fruit and Herb Pimm's or Iced Long Vodka (both page 134) should make a delicious introduction to the party.

mango cheeks with spiced palm sugar ice cream

Palm sugar adds the most wonderful toffee flavour to the ice cream, while star anise offers a hint of something more exotic. This, combined with warm mangoes provides a wickedly delicious pudding.

3 large mangoes
icing sugar, for dusting

spiced palm sugar ice cream
450 ml milk
300 ml double cream
75 g palm sugar, grated, or soft brown sugar
4 whole star anise
5 free range egg yolks

serves 4

To make the ice cream, mix the milk, cream, sugar and star anise into a heavy-based saucepan and heat gently until the mixture just reaches boiling point. Set aside to infuse for 20 minutes. Put the egg yolks into a bowl and beat until pale, then stir in the infused milk. Return to the saucepan and heat gently, stirring constantly, until the mixture is thickened and coats the back of a spoon. Let cool completely, then strain.

Put the mixture into an ice cream machine and freeze according to the manufacturer's instructions. Alternatively, pour into a freezerproof container and freeze for 1 hour until just frozen. Beat vigorously to break up the ice crystals and return to the freezer. Repeat several times until frozen. Soften in the refrigerator for 20 minutes before serving.

Using a sharp knife, cut the cheeks off each mango and put onto a plate. Dust the cut side of each mango cheek with a little icing sugar.

Preheat the barbecue, then grill the cheeks for 2 minutes on each side. Cut the cheeks in half lengthways and serve 3 wedges per person with the ice cream.

barbecued pears with spiced honey, walnuts and blue cheese

A simple but delicious end to a meal – the pears, blue cheese and walnuts perfectly complement one another. Serve on toast with a glass or two of dessert wine. For the best results, choose ripe but firm pears.

50 g walnuts

2 tablespoons clear honey

¼ teaspoon ground cardamom

4 pears

2 tablespoons caster sugar, for dusting

125 g Gorgonzola cheese

to serve

toast

dessert wine

serves 4

Put the walnuts into a frying pan, add the honey and cardamom and cook over a high heat until the honey bubbles furiously and starts to darken. Immediately pour the mixture onto a sheet of greaseproof paper and let cool.

Peel the nuts from the paper and set aside.

Preheat the barbecue. Using a sharp knife, cut the pears into quarters and remove and discard the cores. Cut the pear quarters into thick wedges. Dust lightly with caster sugar and cook over medium hot coals for about 1½ minutes on each side.

Pile the pears onto slices of toast, sprinkle with the walnuts and serve with some Gorgonzola cheese and a glass of dessert wine.

Wrapping fruits in foil is a great way to cook them on the barbecue – all the juices are contained in the parcel while the fruit softens.

grilled fruit parcels

4 peaches or nectarines, halved, stoned and sliced

200 g blueberries

125 g raspberries

juice of 1 orange

1 teaspoon ground cinnamon

2 tablespoons caster sugar

200 g thick yoghurt

1 tablespoon clear honey

1 tablespoon rosewater

1 tablespoon chopped pistachio nuts

serves 4

Put the fruit into a large bowl, add the orange juice, cinnamon and sugar and mix well. Divide the fruit mixture between 4 sheets of foil. Fold the foil over the fruit and seal the edges to make parcels.

Put the yoghurt, honey and rosewater into a separate bowl and mix well. Set aside until required.

Preheat the barbecue, then cook the parcels over medium hot coals for 5–6 minutes. Remove the parcels from the heat, open carefully and transfer to 4 serving bowls. Serve with the yoghurt and a sprinkling of pistachio nuts.

This dish works well with stone fruits too, such as plums, peaches or nectarines.

grilled figs
with almond mascarpone cream

150 g mascarpone cheese

½ teaspoon vanilla essence

1 tablespoon toasted
ground almonds

1 tablespoon Marsala wine

1 tablespoon clear honey

1 tablespoon caster sugar

1 teaspoon ground cardamom

8–10 figs, halved

serves 4

Put the mascarpone cheese, vanilla essence, almonds, Marsala wine and honey into a bowl and beat well. Set aside in the refrigerator until required.

Put the sugar and ground cardamom into a separate bowl and mix well, then carefully dip the cut surface of the figs into the mixture.

Preheat the barbecue, then cook the figs over medium hot coals for 1–2 minutes on each side until charred and softened.

Transfer the grilled figs to 4 serving bowls and serve with the almond mascarpone cream.

This is one for the kids. S'mores are an American campfire classic where graham crackers, barbecued marshmallows and chocolate squares are sandwiched together making a delicious, gooey taste sensation. I prefer to use a sweet biscuit, such as langue du chat or almond thins instead of graham crackers, but any will do.

s'mores

16 biscuits

8 pieces of plain chocolate

16 marshmallows

8 metal skewers

serves 4

Put half the biscuits onto a plate and top each one with a square of chocolate.

Preheat the barbecue. Thread 2 marshmallows onto each skewer and cook over hot coals for about 2 minutes, turning constantly until the marshmallows are melted and blackened. Remove from the heat and let cool slightly.

Put the marshmallows onto the chocolate squares and sandwich together with the remaining biscuits. Gently ease out the skewers and serve the s'mores as soon as the chocolate melts.

iced long vodka

4 shots iced vodka, preferably Absolut

4 shots lime cordial

a few drops of Angostura bitters

to serve

ice cubes

tonic water

1 unwaxed lemon, sliced

serves 4

Vodka and lime is a classic combination and here the drink is given a refreshing twist with the addition of a few drops of Angostura bitters.

Pour the vodka, lime cordial and a little Angostura bitters into 4 tall glasses and add ice cubes and lemon slices. Top up with tonic water and serve.

fruit and herb pimm's

1 bottle Pimm's No 1

250 g strawberries, hulled and halved

½ melon, deseeded and chopped, or nectarine slices

1 unwaxed lemon, sliced

½ cucumber, sliced

a few mint leaves

a few borage flowers (optional)

to serve

ice cubes

1 bottle lemonade or ginger ale

serves 12

A balmy summer's evening seems the perfect time for a glass of Pimm's overflowing with soft fruits and fresh herbs. You can vary the fruits as you wish, but always include some slices of cucumber and a handful of fresh mint leaves.

Pour the Pimm's into a large jug and add the halved strawberries, nectarine slices, lemon slices, cucumber slices and some mint and borage leaves, if using. Set aside to infuse for 30 minutes. Pour into tall glasses filled with ice cubes and top up with lemonade or ginger ale.

strawberry, pear and orange frappé

400 g strawberries, hulled

4 pears, quartered and cored

300 ml freshly squeezed orange juice

ice cubes, to serve (optional)

serves 4

For this fresh juice you really need a juicer, but at a pinch you could purée the fruits in a blender. Always make fresh juices just before serving, because they can discolour and separate quickly.

Push the strawberries and pears through a juicer and transfer to a jug. Add the orange juice and pour into glasses half filled with ice cubes. Serve at once.

ginger and lime cordial

150 g fresh ginger

2 unwaxed limes, sliced

500 g granulated sugar

to serve

ice cubes

unwaxed lime wedges

sparkling water

1 sterilized bottle, 750 ml (page 4)

makes about 750 ml

A lovely refreshing cordial with a delicious kick of ginger – perfect for any occasion.

Using a sharp knife, peel and thinly slice the ginger, then pound lightly with a rolling pin. Put into a saucepan, add the lime slices and 1 litre water, bring to the boil, part-cover with a lid and simmer gently for 45 minutes. Remove from the heat, add the sugar and stir until dissolved. Let cool, strain and pour the cordial into a sterilized bottle. Seal and store until ready to use.

When ready to serve, pour a little cordial into glasses, add ice and lime wedges and top up with sparkling water.

planning the party

For the first barbecue party of the season, I like to wipe down all the exterior surfaces of the barbecue with warm soapy water and make sure that the rack is clean and well oiled. If you have a gas barbecue, fire it up, just to check that everything will be running smoothly on the day.

Number of guests

• Recipes in this book will mostly serve 4, but they can easily be adapted to cater for as many people as you want, simply multiply as required.

• The size of your barbecue and the space available in your garden or terrace may well determine the number of guests you invite.

• Unless you are happy to keep cooking all evening, then work out how many servings you can get onto your barbecue at one time.

• You will need extra chairs and a large table, plus plates, cutlery and glasses. All these things can be hired if you need to.

• Choosing what to cook is the fun part and I like to offer a balance of meat, poultry, fish and seafood, vegetables and vegetarian alternatives.

• Plan well ahead so you can order ingredients in advance. Shop for the non-perishables a week ahead and then many of the raw ingredients can be bought the day before and others picked up early on the day of the party.

• Always check that you have plenty of fuel (unless you have a mains gas or electric grill). Keep a spare full gas bottle or buy double the amount of charcoal you need—you can always use it next time.

Drinks

• Order drinks in advance and don't forget to ask for 'sale or return' – over-order rather than under-order. The same supplier may be used to hire glasses.

• Order lots of non-alcoholic drinks as well, for non-drinkers and children.

• Food and drink must be kept cold, so make as much room in the refrigerator as you can for the food—line up the cool boxes for salads, and hire dustbins or plastic tubs for drinks and fill them up with ice. Have the drinks delivered cold, and pack them in ice as soon as they arrive.

Lights and bugs

• Evening parties need direct lighting for cooking, and moody lights for guests—plenty of night lights, storm lanterns and large candles will add a lovely ambience to the evening.

• Burning citronella candles and mosquito coils will help to keep the bugs at bay.

The one-week guide to a successful barbecue party

The week before
• Stock up on fuel for the barbecue (buy extra) and shop for any non-perishable foods.
• Order drinks and any furniture, china, cutlery and glasses.

The day before

• Buy and prepare meat or fish to be marinated overnight and marinate in the refrigerator.

• Shop for as much remaining food as possible.

• Prepare accompaniments or dressings that keep well overnight.

In the morning

• Collect fresh seafood and any other delicate foods.

• Start marinating any other recipes.

• Prepare as much of the dishes as you can in advance and keep them in the refrigerator or cool place until 1 hour before cooking.

• Set up the tables and chairs and clean the china, cutlery and glasses.

Two hours before

• Set up the bar area and get drinks cooling in the bins or tubs.

• Prepare salads and other last-minute foods, such as kebabs.

• Assemble all the cooking utensils, including roasting tins for resting meat and fish.

One hour and counting

• Return chilled foods to room temperature.

• Soak any wood chips ready for smoking.

• If using charcoal or wood, prepare to light the fuel either with a chimney starter or in the grate.

• Light coals or wood 30 minutes before cooking and light the gas burners 15 minutes before cooking.

• Just before cooking, brush over the grill rack and spray with oil.

• If you will be cooking for longer than an hour you must have a second load of coals or wood ready to go, so prepare the chimney starter and light it up at least 15 minutes before adding the coals to the existing fire.

Cooking

• If you are providing guests with barbecued starters, cook and serve these first. Then you can concentrate on the main course.

• Make sure the coals or burners are hot before you start to cook.

• Because most barbecue foods are best eaten hot, straight from the grill, wait until everyone has finished nibbling the starters before cooking the next course.

• Remember, all cuts of meat and fish are best rested briefly before serving – transfer the cooked foods to the roasting tins for a few minutes.

Finally

• As soon as all the cooking is finished, keep the grill rack over the heat for a few minutes, then rub well with a wire brush to remove as much cooked-on debris as you can.

• Turn off the gas at both the appliance and the bottle or mains or, if using charcoal or wood, let them cool completely.

food and fire safety

Fire safety

• Find a sheltered spot with little or no wind to blow smoke and sparks, but close enough to the kitchen for convenience.

• Choose a flat non-flammable surface, such as a terrace or flat grassy area.

• Avoid a wooden deck as sparks or embers may drop through.

• Never leave hot coals unattended – or food on the grill, for that matter.

• Wear sensible clothes; long trousers and closed sandals are safer for the cook.

• If you've taken your portable barbecue along on a picnic, always avoid areas with dry timbers or long dry grass.

• Let coals cool completely before disposing of them—safely and legally.

• Remember the coals take at least 2 hours to cool sufficiently to be transported safely. It is a good idea to take a heatproof bucket with a lid for this purpose.

Food safety

• Barbecuing is no different from any other cooking when it comes to food safety. To ensure that what we eat is safe for us we must take the steps necessary to avoid food poisoning which, although rarely life-threatening, can be extremely unpleasant. Young children, the elderly, and pregnant women are particularly vulnerable to illness caused by unsafe foods, and the main way that food becomes contaminated is by poor storage or dirty utensils.

• Generally, we tend to barbecue in summer when temperatures are higher, so extra care should be taken keep foods cool. Take a cool box to the shops to transport raw foods, then put them in the refrigerator as soon as possible.

• A refrigerator is the best place to store all perishables and the temperature must be kept between 1–4°C, the recommended range for a domestic refrigerator. Store raw and cooked ingredients on separate shelves to avoid any cross-contamination

• Most of the foods we cook on the barbecue will have started off raw. Although they must be stored in the refrigerator, it is best to return them to room temperature for about 1 hour before cooking. This will ensure that the cooking times given in the recipes are accurate. Once it has reached room temperature, food should be cooked as quickly as possible to prevent it from spoiling.

• If you are marinating something for an hour or less, then it should be fine to do this in a cool place. But if in doubt, refrigerate it.

• If you are travelling any great distance, transport all the perishables in a cool box with several ice packs. Always pack raw or heavy items at the bottom and the more delicate ones at the top.

• Always keep foods covered with clingfilm or a clean cloth while they are waiting to be cooked to keep the bugs away.

• All cooked foods are safest eaten soon after cooking and most barbecued foods are best eaten hot from the fire. If you are barbecuing vegetables to eat later, then cool them as quickly as possible and chill in the refrigerator until required.

• You should always let hot food cool down completely before transferring to the refrigerator, or the interior temperature will rise and put all the contents at risk.

• Remember health issues when cooking pork and poultry, always make sure the meat is totally cooked through before eating. This can be done either by using an instant-read thermometer or by inserting a skewer into the thickest part of the meat. If the juices run clear, the meat is cooked. If they are bloody, return to the barbecue and continue cooking. If you are at home you can always transfer the meat to a preheated oven for the final 10–15 minutes to be safe.

• Make sure that all work surfaces are thoroughly clean before preparing foods. If you are not in a kitchen. remember to take a couple of clean chopping boards with you. Wipe them down well after preparing raw meat – I always take antiseptic wipes with me.

websites and mail order

Most major garden centres, department stores and DIY stores stock a range of barbecues and accessories.

B&Q
Barbecues, charcoal kits, patio heaters, garden lights, charcoal briquettes, lumpwood and accessories.
Call 0845 222 1000 for nearest stockist
www.diy.com

Homebase
Barbecues, accessories, fish baskets, patio heaters, cooler bags, garden lights.
Call 0870 900 8098 for nearest stockist or visit
www.homebase.co.uk

John Lewis
Barbecues and accessories.
Call for nearest stockist
08456 049049 or visit
www.johnlewis.com

Scott & Sargeant Cookshop
*Call 01403 265386 for a free catalogue or visit
www.mycookshop.com*

Websites
Barbecue Online
All the information you need on gas and charcoal barbecues. Lots of tips for successful barbecuing and where to buy gas cylinders in the UK.
www.barbecue-online.co.uk

Barbecues UK
Call 01726 76245 or visit
www.thebbq.co.uk

Flaming Barbecues
Barbecues, patio heaters and smokers.
Call 0800 169 6016 or visit
www.flamingbarbecues.co.uk

Garden Furniture & Barbecues 2 Go
Call 01920 466060 for nearest stockist or visit
www.bbqs2go.co.uk

Garden Site
Barbecues, accessories, plus free advice.
Call 0121 355 7701 for general enquiries or visit
www.gardensite.co.uk

Towler Staines
Call 01535 606631 or visit
www.towler-staines.co.uk

Barbecue Manufacturers
Outback
Good quality Australian-style flat bed and hooded barbecues, available from all major garden centres and department stores.
Call 01622 671771 for nearest stockist or visit
www.outbackuk.com

Weber
Good quality charcoal, gas and portable barbecues, waterproof covers and accessories, including garden lights. All available from garden centres and department stores.
Call 01756 692600 for nearest stockist or visit
www.weber.com

Food Suppliers

Fish
The Fish Society
A huge range of fresh fish including organic and wild salmon, smoked fish and shellfish. Next day delivery.
Call 0800 279 3474 or visit
www.thefishsociety.co.uk

Seafooddirect
*Fish and seafood.
Home delivery.*
Call 01472 210147 or visit
www.seafooddirect.co.uk for a catalogue.

Wing of St Mawes
*Fresh and smoked fish.
Next day home delivery.*
Call 01726 861666 or visit
www.cornish-seafood.co.uk

Poultry and Meat
The Country Butcher
Award-winning sausages and traditional bacon. Mail order.
Call 01452 831023 or visit
www.countrybutcher.co.uk

Providence Farm Organic Meats
A variety of organic meat including pork, beef, chicken and duck. Mail order.
Call 01409 254421 or visit
www.providencefarm.co.uk

Blackmount Foods
Organic meat including beef, lamb, pork, chicken. Mail order.
Call 01899 221747 or visit
www.blackmountfoods.com

Miscellaneous
Extra Virgin Olive Oils and Mediterranean Foods
Olive oils and Mediterranean produce. Mail order.
Call 01460 72931 or visit
www.getoily.com

Graig Farm Organics
Extensive range of organic fish, dairy produce, groceries, fruit, vegetables and organic alcohol. Mail order.
Call 01597 851655 or visit
www.graigfarm.co.uk

The Spice Shop
Freshly ground spices, spice blends and herbs. Mail order.
Call 0207 221 4448 or visit
www.thespiceshop.co.uk

Kitchenware and utensils

Divertimenti
Two shops in London, plus mail order catalogue.
33–34 Marylebone High Street
London W1U 4PT
Tel: 020 7935 0689
www.divertimenti.co.uk

Lakeland Limited
Equipment available by mail order, on line, and from their many shops. Phone for details.
Alexandra Buildings
Windermere,
Cumbria CA23 1BQ
Tel 015394 88100
www.lakelandlimited.com

index